Nenilava, Prophetess of Madagascar

Nenilava, Prophetess of Madagascar

Her Life and the Ongoing Revival She Inspired

James B. Vigen
AND
Sarah Hinlicky Wilson

☙PICKWICK *Publications* · Eugene, Oregon

NENILAVA, PROPHETESS OF MADAGASCAR
Her Life and the Ongoing Revival She Inspired

Copyright © 2021 James B. Vigen and Sarah Hinlicky Wilson. All rights reserved. Except for brief quotations in critical publications or reviews, no part of this book may be reproduced in any manner without prior written permission from the publisher. Write: Permissions, Wipf and Stock Publishers, 199 W. 8th Ave., Suite 3, Eugene, OR 97401.

Pickwick Publications
An Imprint of Wipf and Stock Publishers
199 W. 8th Ave., Suite 3
Eugene, OR 97401

www.wipfandstock.com

PAPERBACK ISBN: 978-1-7252-7327-6
HARDCOVER ISBN: 978-1-7252-7328-3
EBOOK ISBN: 978-1-7252-7329-0

Cataloguing-in-Publication data:

Names: Vigen, James B., author. | Wilson, Sarah Hinlicky, author.

Title: Nenilava, prophetess of Madagascar : her life and the ongoing revival she inspired / by James B. Vigen and Sarah Hinlicky Wilson.

Description: Eugene, OR : Pickwick Publications, 2021 | Includes bibliographical references.

Identifiers: ISBN 978-1-7252-7327-6 (paperback) | ISBN 978-1-7252-7328-3 (hardcover) | ISBN 978-1-7252-7329-0 (ebook)

Subjects: LCSH: Christianity—Madagascar. | Madagascar—Church history.

Classification: BR1470.M2 V55 2021 (print) | BR1470.M2 V55 (ebook)

11/18/21

Scripture quotations are from The ESV® Bible (The Holy Bible, English Standard Version®), copyright © 2001 by Crossway, a publishing ministry of Good News Publishers. Used by permission. All rights reserved.

Contents

A Note on Malagasy Names | vii

Introduction by Sarah Hinlicky Wilson | 1

Chapter 1: The History of the Ankaramalaza Revival (1941–1970) by Zakaria Tsivoery | 6

Chapter 2: The Rest of the Story (1971–1998) by James B. Vigen | 72

Chapter 3: Interpretation, Analysis, and Appreciation of Nenilava and Her Movement by James B. Vigen | 83

Conclusion by Sarah Hinlicky Wilson | 114

Bibliography | 135

A Note on Malagasy Names

BETSY RYMES HAS OBSERVED about Madagascar: "[F]rom an anthropological perspective, names are not simply arbitrary labels. How we get them, who says them, how they are used, and in what context they are spoken are inseparable from a human being's social identity. . . . [T]he Malagasy of Madagascar . . . recognize the power of individuals' names and use them scrupulously, preferring to avoid using birth names at all. . . . Their beliefs regarding the use of names by ancestral forces led the Malagasy to change their names so many times that the name's pragmatic referential purpose was being subverted and a national law (limiting the number of name changes to seven) was put into effect to curb confusion."[1]

Surnames are not mandatory in Madagascar. There is no set custom of having a "family" or patronymic name, though in the current generation some people are trying to establish that pattern. In Madagascar it is still legal for a person to have only one name, though it is more common to have three or even four names. If, following the Western convention, a person has a French or Western name, it is written first and the Malagasy name or names second. But if one follows the original Malagasy convention, then the Malagasy name comes first, with any Western name second or in last place. For example, during the time that the past president of the Malagasy Lutheran Church was a graduate student in the United States, he was required to list his name as Modeste Endor Rakoto, but in Madagascar he is known as Rakoto Endor Modeste.

---

1. Rymes, "Names," 163, 164–65.

A NOTE ON MALAGASY NAMES

   Malagasy names are given to show lineage, to indicate parents' wishes for their child, and to signify an important event in the life of the family. For example, if a couple had a child with the given name *Tiana* ("beloved") who subsequently died, the next child might be named *Solotiana*, "in place of Tiana."

   Given the stakes in Malagasy culture, therefore, we have in this book presented Malagasy names as the Malagasy themselves do.

Introduction

—Sarah Hinlicky Wilson

I FIRST BECAME AWARE of Madagascar during my childhood through photos of its strange and wondrous animals, and not, like the generation after me, through a Disney movie of the same name that has nothing whatsoever to do with the island nation.

Many, many years after my first glimpses of lemurs and chameleons, in 2013, I met my first Malagasy in person, Toromaree Mananato. She was a participant in the annual Studying Luther in Wittenberg seminar that I have taught every November since 2009 with Theodor Dieter, my colleague at the Institute for Ecumenical Research in Strasbourg, France. Toromaree was present at the behest of the Malagasy Lutheran Church (MLC), where she was serving as the national secretary of the women's association (and soon to be vice-general secretary of the MLC). When she told me where she was from, I mentioned the animal pictures I'd seen and how I'd always thought Madagascar would be an interesting place to visit. She said, without skipping a beat, "OK! I'll invite you!" Three days later I had a letter from Rakoto Endor Modeste, president of the MLC, asking me to come and teach a weeklong course at the Lutheran Graduate School of Theology in Ivory, Fianarantsoa.

By this time I knew that there was a sizable Lutheran church in Madagascar, with a membership of at least four million, which struck me as almost as strange and wondrous as the lemurs and chameleons. My first encounter with Lutheran missions to Madagascar came through none other than James B. Vigen, my co-author on this volume. I met him in circumstances that in no way forecast our eventual collaboration: he had just returned from Madagascar and was serving a congregation in the city where my grandmother was dying an untimely death. I was in college at the time; I have a blurry but grateful memory of Vigen's kind ministrations to my family while we were beside ourselves with shock and grief. Having now lived abroad and repatriated a few times myself, I can only imagine his own disorientation at being back in the United States after eighteen years in Madagascar.

In any event, by the time I was preparing for my visit to teach in Madagascar in the fall of 2014—a trip on which my husband Andrew L. Wilson would accompany me as co-teacher, and also our son and my husband's parents—I had gotten up to speed on the Lutheranism of Madagascar. It arose in the late nineteenth century due to missions from both Norwegians and Norwegian-Americans. To hear the Malagasy tell it, the principal difference between them was that the former forbade beer while the latter allowed it in moderation! Whatever the inevitable strains between missionaries and locals, the cooperation was sufficiently strong over the succeeding decades to have all but eclipsed a pattern seen much more commonly on the continent of Africa, namely the departure of the recipients of missions to establish independent churches, "African-Initiated Churches" as they are often called. By and large Malagasy Christians adhere to the historic churches that brought the gospel to them: in addition to Lutherans there are many Roman Catholics, Reformed, and Anglicans, as well as assorted other traditions and denominations.

Two things in particular impressed me about Malagasy Lutheranism and elicited further interest. First was the fact that "revival" (*fifohazana* in Malagasy) was not only well-integrated into a tradition that I thought, based on my own experience, to be anathema to revivalism of any kind, but that the MLC had undergone *four* revivals already in its short existence—the first only thirty years after the first Lutheran missionaries arrived—and that all four revivals were still alive in one form or another! Clearly, this was not the circus tent or anxious bench of the American awakenings. My notion of "revival" and its relationship to the institution of the church needed serious reconsideration.

And second was the fact that you could not talk about Malagasy Lutheranism or its revivals at all without talking about Nenilava.

Here again I'd heard just enough to know that I should ask about Nenilava when I arrived in Madagascar. Béatrice Bengtsson at the Lutheran World Federation, where Malagasy pastor and scholar Péri Rasolondraibe had recently left a ten-year stint as director of the department for mission and development, told me how he always spoke passionately of Nenilava's formative impact on his life and work. Others mentioned to me—or maybe they were trying to warn me?—that Nenilava had been an exorcist, and how that was still a major aspect of religious practice in Malagasy Lutheranism. Needless to say, I touched down in Antananarivo anxious to learn more!

It is no exaggeration to say that I felt Nenilava's presence everywhere. The first and most obvious sign was, in fact, a sign. A plaque at the MLC compound in the Isoraka neighborhood of the capital honors her by her given name, "Volahavana Germaine, Revival Leader," alongside memorials to other foreign missionaries and local luminaries in the history of the MLC. My family and I were taken to the healing camp at Ambohibao-Antehiroka (the successor to the *toby* initially located at 67 Hectares) that Nenilava founded and saw both where she lived and the current patients in residence at the *toby*.

Once we got to Fianarantsoa and had a week with students, I asked them what, if anything, they knew about her. Everyone had a story! One told me how she had arranged the match between his parents, which I later learned was one of her many ministerial interventions in people's lives. Nearly all the students I met were shepherd-exorcists (*mpiandry* in Malagasy) in the Ankaramalaza revival tradition—only later would I meet church leaders who came from the other strands of revival—and they talked joyfully of the kind of ministry they did, which most certainly included exorcism. My husband and I attended two worship services that included the spiritual work (*asa* in Malagasy) that characterizes the *mpiandry* of Ankaramalaza. One of the services took place at a prison and was attended by about half the male inmates (and a very bare minimum of security guards). The other was a standard weekday worship service, at which the *mpiandry* made me, along with the rest of the congregation, recipient of the exorcistic action!

The fascination with Nenilava stayed with me, but I did not expect to visit Madagascar again after that. My family moved back to the States from France, and then from the States to Japan, and there is a limit to the number of countries and churches one can keep an eye on. However, even after leaving my full-time position at the Institute for Ecumenical Research, I have remained a consultant to the International Lutheran-Pentecostal Dialogue and taken part in its annual meetings. And so it was in this capacity that I made my second trip to Madagascar in the fall of 2019.

In retrospect I can see that my first trip was nonstop shock at the new: from the poverty to the exorcisms to the, yes, strange and wondrous animals. I'm glad I had the opportunity to visit a second time, because it allowed me to see differently and, I hope, to understand better what I saw. And it certainly helped that the very reason our dialogue team chose Madagascar as a destination was because the MLC subverts both Lutheran and Pentecostal expectations about the boundaries between our theological traditions and worship practices. To Pentecostals it said: a church can be charismatic *and also* confessional; to the Lutherans it said: a church can be confessional *and also* charismatic. During this second visit, I attended several more worship services led by *mpiandry* from the Ankaramalaza revival that Nenilava founded, and I found in the MLC bookstore a French translation of Zakaria Tsivoery's biography of Nenilava. That was the seed of the book you are reading today.

If you have made it this far into the Introduction, then presumably you have sufficient curiosity to overcome the bewilderment and alarm that inevitably follows Westerners' contact with these rather typical practices of African Christianity. As Jesus pointed out, you know the tree by its fruits. While the potential for and reality of abuse certainly exists wherever great power, and especially great spiritual power, is at work, the fact remains that Nenilava's ministry and its outgrowths have done enormous good—*good* as defined by the gospel of Jesus Christ.

For this reason, Vigen and I have undertaken to bring, for the first time, a detailed account of Nenilava and her revival to an English-speaking audience. While some books and scholarly articles deal with her in passing (see the Bibliography), ours presents the first English translation of the closest thing we have to a firsthand account of her life and work, namely the aforementioned biography written by Zakaria Tsivoery, a pastor of the MLC to whom Nenilava entrusted her story. I made a complete translation of the French text into English and sent it on to Vigen to see if he'd be interested in coediting a volume about her, centered on this text. He had a copy of the Malagasy original and, in reviewing my translation, discovered certain liberties taken in the French translation. As a result, Vigen ended up going through my entire translation line by line to make it adhere more closely to the Malagasy original, and that is the version presented here.

Tsivoery's account ends in the early 1970s, but Nenilava did not die until 1998. Therefore, to supplement the biography, Vigen scouted out primary sources in Malagasy to bring the story to its conclusion, which he reports in the second section of this book. In the third section, he expands the story to include the Ankaramalaza revival more broadly and its impact on the MLC, Madagascar as a whole, and the church throughout the world.

We hope this book can serve as the primary source on Nenilava and the Ankaramalaza revival for the anglophone audience.

However, given what I've already reported here about Nenilava, a mere recounting of the facts as they have been passed along is insufficient. A further step needs to be taken toward interpreting those facts for a Western readership. Therefore, in the final section of this book, I will take up a number of neuralgic issues raised by the history of Nenilava: questions about evil spirits, miracles, healing and sin, emergent offices of ministry, and implications for Christians in the Western world.

But, for now, you should simply enjoy the ride through Nenilava's astonishing life story!

Chapter 1: The History of the Ankaramalaza Revival (1941–1970)

—Zakaria Tsivoery

Preface

Dear readers, I had no intention at all of writing this history of the spiritual revival that relates to Volahavana Germaine ("Nenilava"). My motivation was the fruit of our meeting during her visit to Fort Dauphin in November 1963.

A short time after our conversation, I approached her and asked whether I could write the story of her calling from God. She told me that others had gathered material about it, but they had not distributed it to others, keeping it to themselves. Other writings appeared in the church magazine *Ny Mpamangy*, then in the book entitled *Réveil spirituel à Madagascar* ("Spiritual Revival in Madagascar"), written by Rajosefa Danielson, a retired pastor of Vatotsara, Madagascar. In fact, all these writings were incomplete and only tell certain parts of her story. But if you feel the need to write my history, she said to me, I will have the pleasure of delivering it to you. She let me know that it was not for her sake that she was authorizing me to publish her history, but because she was persuaded of the fact that the hearing and reading of these stories would do good, and no harm, to Christians.

I have well perceived the veracity of these tales in hearing them told: my heart was touched. Similarly, I believe that others' hearts will also be touched in hearing and reading her history. This is what pushed me to make the decision to write and offer to you, dear readers, what I have received from Nenilava.

May God accompany you in your reading and may your life change, to the glory of God our Father alone.

Your friend,
Pastor Zakaria Tsivoery
Fort Dauphin

I. The Parents of Germaine Volahavana ("Nenilava")

Germaine Volahavana was the daughter of Malady and Vao, who lived in Mandrondra, in the canton of Lakomby, which is in the district of Manakara. Their ancestral people group are the Antaimoro. Malady was a *mpanjaka* [petty king] of this clan and an *ombiasa* [diviner-healer] of great renown in his region.

Because of Malady's fame, people came from all around to consult him. They came asking for wealth, a herd of zebu, or for children, for they believed in his powers. Because of the power of darkness at work in him, he was said to know in advance who it was that would come to him and why. Every time someone approached him seeking help, he practiced his *sikidy* [a form of divination by casting special stones or seeds and reading them].

Germaine Volahavana saw all these people who came to see her father. She watched her father closely during these consultations and observed the manner in which they proceeded. Each time that Malady indulged in his *sikidy*, he said that the charms were gods or spirits [*andriamanitra*]. From her earliest childhood, Germaine Volahavana did not like either divination or idolatry.

Every time her father engaged in his divination sessions, she would say, "Where is this god to whom you speak with your charms? For I don't like a god who cannot speak, who always needs a 'mouth-piece'; and besides, God cannot be seen." She often made such comments to her father's face, even doing so in front of those who had come seeking his services, which made her father very angry with her.

When she reached the age of seventeen, several suitors came to ask for her hand in marriage. She rejected all these offers of marriage because it had never crossed her mind to get married. When her father saw the character of her spirit, he was astounded and saddened, because these people whom she had rejected could have given her a peaceful life.

Her parents just didn't understand how their daughter could refuse all these men who would have supported her and given her a peaceful life. So Malady gathered all of his children together and told them that Germaine must be possessed by a kind of spirit that considered her to be its own wife. That must be why she refused all marriage offers made to her! Therefore he consulted his charms. When he did so, Malady was quite shaken, for he had never before in his whole life seen such a thing. The charms had spoken to him and revealed that a great spirit, who is a great God, dwelt in Germaine and that is what caused her to refuse marriage altogether. But what totally amazed her father was what else he saw revealed by the charms. The charms said to him that he was a slave, but Germaine Volahavana was a queen.

This revelation completely amazed him, because what could possibly make his daughter a queen except that she had inherited the office from her father? On the other hand, if the father was a slave, that would make his daughter a slave also. Yet that was not what was revealed by his charms; rather, that he was a servant, while his daughter was a queen. What made his daughter a queen, her father decided, was because of the Spirit of God that was in her.

Thus Malady declared to all his children that the God of Volahavana was the one true God and above all the other gods whom he had served. "So, I order all of my children to serve and follow this God. Those who do not follow him will be lost and will die eternally. And, from now on until my death, I will no longer engage in divination with my charms. Furthermore, I announce to you that two years after the rule [or spiritual work] of Volahavana has begun, I will die."

The words of her father came true, for two years after Germaine Volahavana began her work, her father died. This caused some persons not to believe that Germaine Volahavana was a messenger of God. They thought instead that the spirit that dwelt in her father had simply been passed on to live in her. This is not true, however, according to what we have seen in her and because of what we know of her spiritual works and her full and powerful preaching of the word of God, for the Lord worked in her. "And they went out and preached everywhere, while the Lord worked with them and confirmed the message by accompanying signs" (Mark 16:20).

II. Her Childhood and the Origin of the Voice That Called to Her

During the whole of her childhood, Volahavana was raised in the pagan environment of her parents. She was not yet a Christian when she received the call of God into his service. She was only ten years old at the time that Jesus chose her for his service.

From then on she had frequent dreams. In one of them, every evening a white man led her into a large building made of stone. One time she found herself alone in front of the building while the man who accompanied her slipped away. A little while later, though, he came back with a bucket full of water. He then poured the water into a great basin. Next he raised Germaine Volahavana by her hands and placed her in the middle of the basin filled with water and washed her feet. When he had finished, he took a towel and dried her feet. Finally, he raised her again by the hands and laid her down on a bed that he then rocked gently until she fell asleep. Such was the nature of her dream, which repeated itself more than once.

Another dream told of a person who caught her up in a big net and lifted her up to heaven. This dream also repeated itself several times. These two dreams came back to her regularly until she was twelve years old. From that time on her dreams ceased, but a new thing came along: Jesus called her by name. She did not at first realize, though, that it was Jesus who was calling to her; she simply heard his voice.

At that time, Jesus began his work in her and began to do amazing things through her. If, for example, a person began to talk about her or to gossip about her, Jesus told her who was doing it and what they said. She often dared to approach the person and tell them everything that they had said about her! The person in question would be astonished to hear it and asked her, "Who told you these things?" Volahavana would only laugh while not revealing who had told her.

Volahavana didn't play with other children either in the daytime or in the evenings. She isolated herself and cried a lot. She seemed joyless and miserable in her heart and was always sad. Her friends were always amusing themselves with their games at night, while Volahavana would instead take a large wooden mortar for the pounding of rice and sit on it outside to gaze, captivated, at the brilliance of the stars. She wondered to herself, "When will I have the chance to see God?"

Volahavana ardently desired God with all her heart and aspired to rise up to heaven. And so, she said to herself, "I am going to make a ladder, putting wooden planks end to end, and once the ladder is finished, I will climb up and see God! It is clear that it was this dream that caused her lack of enthusiasm for playing with her friends, for she feared that if she did she would not be able to discern properly the voice that spoke to her.

Volahavana created her own special place under the roots of a large tree, and after cleaning the area thoroughly she cried out, "I really want to meet you, O God, if you are willing to show yourself to people." Her abundant tears wore her out and she fell asleep under the tree in her special place.

All this time her parents were searching hard to find her. They finally located her at the foot of the tree and reprimanded her, saying, "Have you gone mad to act this way?" By now she was no longer crying but laughed at her parents' words. Every time she thought about going out to play with her friends, a voice would interrupt her thoughts, speaking her name: "Volahavana!" The voice called to her in this way every day at noon. When she heard the voice, she would run to her parents and say to them, "Is it you who called me?" Her parents answered, "Are you crazy? Who is calling you?" When she heard her parents say that, she felt wretched and went back outside.

When Volahavana was thirteen, the voice calling her at noon stopped, but the dreams came back again. In her dream, she saw Jesus lead her into a large church. Jesus set her on a chair in the front row of the church. The faithful arrived in such numbers that the church soon was full. Then Jesus took her by the hand and led her into the pulpit. Jesus refused to allow anyone else into the empty place left for Volahavana and put a white cloth there instead.

When the two of them had gone into the pulpit, it was Jesus who preached the word of God to the faithful, leaving Volahavana standing by his side. Jesus told her that she would one day preach in the very same way. When the sermon was over, Jesus led her down from the pulpit and brought her back to her place. Then those assembled there sang hymns. When the service ended, Germaine Volahavana came back to her senses, startled by her dream.

Dreams like this continued for a year. Once again all these kinds of dreams ceased when she reached fourteen years of age, but the voice that had called to her by name at noon every day returned. This went on for a year. Nothing else of note happened apart from the intervention of this voice each day at noon.

When Volahavana turned fifteen, both the dreams and the voice ceased. She passed through a quiet year without anything unusual happening. Jesus seemed to have fallen silent. At that time, men came to her parents asking permission to marry her. Volahavana refused because she had no interest in getting married. Her parents didn't know what to make of her refusal of marriage, so they forced her to go and live with her sister in Manakara.

Volahavana was then sixteen years old. The voice that called to her previously resumed. By seventeen years of age, she told her sister that she had decided to return to the countryside so that she wouldn't be tempted by the ways of the big city.

Three months after Volahavana moved back to the countryside, a widower named Mosesy Tsirefo asked her again to marry him. He was a catechist and had many children from his first wife. As expected, Volahavana refused to marry this man, for marriage had never attracted her before and she had given her heart completely to the one who had called to her. At this time, though, Volahavana was not yet a Christian and she was totally ignorant about Jesus, who was the source of her calling.

Her father, however, forced Volahavana to marry Mosesy Tsirefo whether she liked it or not. So, because of parental pressure and despite her reticence, she consented to marry the catechist.

Volahavana's wedding to the catechist took place in 1935. After the civil wedding, she remained with her parents in order to learn the catechism in preparation for baptism. Two weeks of instruction sufficed for her to be approved for baptism at Lokomby, which in turn allowed for the church blessing to be given on her marriage. Despite the brevity of her time of instruction, Volahavana knew all of her lessons very well. She took the name of Germaine at the time of her baptism. From then on she was known as and called Germaine Volahavana.

However, when she began her ministry she came to be called Nenilava and is so called even till now. The origin and the reason for this name will be explained a bit later in the story.

Ramasivelo was at this time pastor of the Lokomby parish; it was he who performed Volahavana's baptism. After the baptism, her husband took her to live at Ankaramalaza. Her catechist husband continued to instruct her in the Christian faith; the pastors Rakotovao and Bernard Radafy assisted in her instruction. Her married home was a place prepared for her beforehand by God to educate and protect her. She remained there for ten years with Mosesy Tsirefo before he died.

Rev. Listor was the missionary in that area then. Before her baptism, Volahavana had been touched by the Revival movement, even though her Gentile status meant she still did not fully comprehend the scope of her life's mission.

III. The Early Days of Nenilava's Work

At eighteen years of age, Nenilava continued to hear the voice that spoke to her every day at noon, as previously mentioned. In May 1941 Jesus said to Germaine Volahavana in a vision: "Arise, you three sisters: Rasoalina (Ambaniandro), Razafy (Betsileo), and Germaine Volahavana (Antaimoro)."[1] The three sisters immediately got up, as seen in Nenilava's vision. When they rose up to heaven, there was a person there who gave each of them a small white piece of paper to carry along with them. This person advised them to guard the paper given to them well and not to lose it, because they would need to show it if anyone asked them about it along their way.

There were seven portals that had to be passed through before reaching heaven. Each portal had its own guardian. When the women came to the first portal, the guardian asked them, "Where are you going?" They each showed him their respective papers that they were told to carry with them. After each had shown her paper, the guardian of the gate allowed all three of them to enter through it. (I asked Nenilava the reason for this little paper each of them was told to carry with them. Germaine Volahavana explained to me that the reason for this little piece of paper was because on it was written the number of the room where each of them was to be housed once they got to heaven. Only those who carried such a paper were given permission to pass through the gateway by its guardian, as already stated; this was the case at each portal.)

When they arrived at the seventh portal, a young woman welcomed them, saying, "So, you've arrived? Enter into that house down there, and each of you go to your own room." Rasoalina chose the room situated at the north end of the house, Razafy the middle room, and Germaine Volahavana

---

1. Each Malagasy word in parentheses indicates one of the people groups in Madagascar. The Ambaniandro are from Imerina, the region around the national capital; the Betsileo are originally from the province of Fianarantsoa, south of the capital; and the Antaimoro are from the southeast coast.

the one on the south end of the house. Magnificent music and hymns filled their rooms; it was simply incomparable to anything they had ever heard. They looked around, hoping to see the singers, but in vain. They could only hear the music.

Each of the rooms was furnished. They found various items of furniture and utensils there: a golden bowl, a golden spoon, a golden chair and a bed of gold. The bed was like a living thing, for it seemed to breathe. All of these items of gold in each room caused joy and happiness to those who sat upon them. All the golden furniture and utensils symbolized the fact that everything belongs to God. There were many chairs in heaven, each of which belonged to someone of distinction. They were also shown the chair of Judas. It was not nicely positioned like the other chairs but flipped upside down, and there was no one to occupy it. Besides that, there were many other chairs that were also placed upside down. Jesus said that those chairs must not be put back in place; they had to be left like they were so that everyone could see them; and that no one could ever sit on them again because they belonged to traitors. The reason they were shown these chairs was so that they could tell people about them and that it might serve as a lesson for many.

Then they were invited to descend back down to earth in order to begin their spiritual work. After seeing all of this and hearing all that she had heard in heaven, Nenilava got to feeling at home there and didn't want to go back to earth! Jesus had to demand that she go back because she had work to do for which she had been called. When she made only hesitant steps forward, Jesus revealed to her the fires of hell. That's where you will end up, Jesus said, if you do not follow my command to return! Then a person was thrown into the abyss of hell. Nenilava trembled when she saw the flames, the groans, and the complaints of the many people who were suffering there, crying out and saying, "We are dead! We are dead! We are burning up! We are burning up!" She could imagine herself being in the same place as those who were tormented and in agony. When she saw this, Nenilava said to Jesus: "I agree to go!"

After they returned to earth, Jesus instructed the women not to forget about the paper that had been entrusted to each of them and not to lose it. As they were going on their way, Nenilava recalled everything she had seen in her vision. Three months after this vision, Rasoalina died. Razafy, however, did not agree with the work for which she had been called, nor did she ever set foot in a church again, from that time onward, because she simply did not accept the words revealed to her by Germaine Volahavana. By contrast, Germaine Volahavana immediately began to do her spiritual work, as will be presented in what follows in this story.

On Tuesday July 30, 1941, God caused the awakening of Petera, the catechist in Vohidravy. Petera was at home when, suddenly, he began to tremble so much that it was frightening to watch. He asked what was happening to him but no one could answer and no one spoke. His shaking was so strong that the whole house shook also. By chance, the young daughter of Mosesy Tsirefo was sick with fever—this was his second-born daughter. She had an evil spirit living within her; this was why she was sick. Petera began to engage in spiritual work to cast the demon out of this young woman. This spiritual work was very, very difficult, for the demon would not come out of her as commanded. Petera refused to be discouraged but fought and struggled with the evil spirit.

From early in the morning Petera fought with this evil spirit, but around ten o'clock the evil spirit forced the girl out into the forest and made her strip off all her clothes so that she was naked. Germaine Volahavana was obliged to go with her out into the forest and didn't come back with her until three o'clock in the afternoon. The next day, Petera continued to work on casting out the evil spirit from the young girl. Germaine Volahavana was also present in the house during that time. She sat by the fire busily preparing the noon meal, blowing on the fire. Petera labored all alone, trying to expel the demons from this young child, and the work continued to be difficult.

Just then someone behind her lightly touched Germaine Volahavana on the shoulder and said, "Rise up and act!" Surprised and afraid, Nenilava was paralyzed in place and didn't dare to turn around and see who it was that had touched her. When she did sneak a peek behind her, she was astonished to see a very tall man standing there behind her. She wondered to herself, "Who is this man? Could this be Jesus?" The voice did not cease to command her to go and engage in spiritual work with this child. Finally, the man began to tap his foot on the floor and said again, "Rise up and work with this child!"

Germaine Volahavana could not remember what, exactly, she did then or how she got to where the child was, for it was like she was compelled by a force that carried her and pushed her to where the child was, and she entered into the struggle. After she had struggled long and mightily for the child, the devil that was in her said, "We are cast out, we are cast out, for the one who is mightier than we has come!" Then this little girl was healed, and she realized she needed to put her clothes back on. Wednesday August 1, 1941, was the beginning of this spiritual work.

This is a famous date, celebrated every year at the *toby* or spiritual center of Ankaramalaza. On Wednesday night, shortly before dawn on August 2, Jesus said to them, "Rise up, preach the good news everywhere! Cast out the demons. Do your spiritual work, do not delay! The hour has come when the Son of Man must be glorified among all the peoples of Matitanana and Ambohibe. I have chosen you all for this work. This I command you all to do."

Petera and Moses Tsirefo easily agreed to do as Jesus commanded and to go forward in their call, but Germaine Volahavana did not agree to it and was even disposed to reject it outright. Here are the reasons for her refusal: she was still quite young at that time, and she was afraid lest she should bring opposition to the revival. Also, being illiterate and largely untrained in the holy Scriptures, she would not be able to preach. So she told Jesus about her inability to serve in this way. Jesus did not agree and compelled her anyway, saying: "Rise up, proclaim the good news everywhere!" Faced with Jesus' insistence, she could no longer refuse her calling. But she told Jesus that if he didn't reveal to her in advance what she should say to people, she wouldn't have anything at all to say to them! To this Jesus consented. From then on he would reveal to her the things that she should say. When she began her work he labored beside her husband, Mosesy Tsirefo, who died in the year 1949.

When she began the work to which Jesus called her, she was called by the name Nenilava. This name, however, wasn't her real name, as we have seen previously in this story, but Volahavana, or Germaine Volahavana after her baptism.

So, then, where did this name Nenilava come from? This name came from ill-intentioned people, but she accepted it as a mark of honor and it became precious to her. The way this all came about was that there were three people who were all awakened at about the same time: Petera, the catechist at Vohidravy; Mosesy Tsirefo; and Germaine Volohavana herself. Petera was the first to be awakened and began to do the spiritual work of the revival. Because he had begun the work, many people joined him and worked with him. Not long afterwards, Germaine Volahavana began the work to which Jesus had called her. At that time she and Petera worked together. Sadly, later on some of those in Petera's group became jealous of

Germaine Volohavana and even came to hate her. They poured scorn on her and made defamatory remarks about her to try and make her angry. Germaine Volahavana endured all this and did not reply in kind to them, because Jesus forbade her from doing so.

These activities continued and even got worse every time the followers of Petera saw Germaine Volahavana, whether at the church meetings or while they did their everyday work. One day, because of their hearts filled with malice and jealousy, they refused even to speak or pronounce the name of Germaine because they disliked her so. On account of this, they looked for a derogatory nickname for her. But what should they call her? One of them remarked on her height, for she was taller than most people. So they threw out the idea of calling her *Neny-lava* ("tall-mother") on account of her height. They all agreed, and that was how they all came to call her Nenilava. However, she came to love the name above all others, even her given name that she had previously used.

So throughout the island and abroad, she is known by the name of Nenilava. But when Jesus converses with her, he uses the name "Ana." Only Jesus knows the reason for this.[2]

One day Jesus called her because he wanted to give her something. Jesus placed before her three things. These things were arranged before her, and then Jesus and the angel Gabriel stood on the opposite side of these things and offered them to Nenilava. This is what the three things were: first, there was a bright red ball. The second thing was also a ball, but very white. The third thing was a chubby and charming baby!

Standing before her and pointing to these things, the angel Gabriel said to her, "Choose the one that you prefer!" Nenilava hesitated to make a choice for just one of the three things. But she had to indicate her preference according to what the angel said. So, in the end, she got down on her knees to pray and looked to Jesus. The angel Gabriel addressed her again, "Choose now which one of the three you prefer!" So she chose the white ball in the middle and cradled it in her arms. When the angel Gabriel saw this, he asked her again, "Is that really the one that you most want?" Nenilava responded, saying, "It is, sir, what I most want." Then Jesus and Gabriel looked at each other and just smiled.

Nenilava said to the two of them, "I ask you, please explain to me the meaning of these remaining things." Jesus explained them to her, and this

---

2. "Ana" could be short for the Malagasy *anaka*, which means "child." However, the more common word would be *zanaka*.

is what he said: "The red ball represents the world. The white ball, which you have chosen, symbolizes the Holy Spirit. And the third is the gift that is given to humanity to bring joy to them." Then Jesus said to her, "Do you not love this child?" "Yes, I do love it," she said, "but it is something I will need later on."

Nenilava did not have any children, so Jesus gave her the promise contained in Isaiah 54:1–10:

> "Sing, O barren one, who did not bear a child, break forth into singing and cry aloud, you who have not been in labor! For the children of the desolate one will be more than the children of her who is married," says the Lord. "Enlarge the place of your tent, and let the curtains of your habitations be stretched out; do not hold back; lengthen your cords and strengthen your stakes. For you will spread abroad to the right and to the left, and your offspring will possess the nations and will people the desolate cities. Fear not, for you will not be ashamed; be not confounded, for you will not be disgraced; for you will forget the shame of your youth, and the reproach of your widowhood you will remember no more. For your Maker is your husband, the Lord of hosts is his name; and the Holy One of Israel is your redeemer, the God of the whole earth he is called. For the Lord has called you like a wife deserted and grieved in spirit, like a wife of youth when she is cast off, says your God. For a brief moment I deserted you, but with great compassion I will gather you. In overflowing anger, for a moment, I hid my face from you, but with everlasting love I will have compassion on you," says the Lord, your Redeemer. "This is like the days of Noah to me: as I swore that the waters of Noah should no more go over the earth, so I have sworn that I will not be angry with you, and will not rebuke you. For the mountains may depart and the hills be removed, but my steadfast love shall not depart from you and my covenant of peace shall not be removed," says the Lord, who has compassion on you.

When Nenilava reached the age of nineteen, the voice that had always called to her at midday ceased completely, but then Jesus appeared to her directly. Nevertheless, she heard different voices in the air, such that she had difficulties differentiating the voice of Jesus. Furthermore, visions came to her often.

Because of this, she asked Jesus to give her signs so that she could recognize if it really was Jesus who appeared to her, or another. Jesus told her that each time he manifested himself to her, he would show her the holes in his hands, for no one could imitate those, Jesus said! And, in case he could not come to her, he would send an angel that would carry a white cross in its hand.

IV. The Time of Education

Two things Jesus taught Nenilava: to speak in tongues and to know the holy Scriptures.

i. The Teaching about Speaking in Tongues

Speaking in tongues was the first thing that Jesus taught her, because this was to be the language used during her instruction in the holy Scriptures while she was in heaven. The course of study lasted three months.

This is how Jesus taught her. He had a white board that hung on the wall of the house where she was taught. On this white board Jesus wrote the words that he wanted to teach her. The writing on this white board was also in white. Jesus' method of writing was not as we would write, from left to right, but from the top to the bottom, vertically, like the Chinese.

Jesus waited until Mosesy Tsirefo had gone to work in the coffee fields before he came into the house to teach Nenilava. The French language was the first language Jesus taught her. Jesus would pronounce a word first, and then she would repeat it. Then Jesus invited her to have conversations with him in French. As Jesus and Nenilava conversed in the house, Mosesy could hear them, for the coffee field that he was hoeing was located not far from the house. Mosesy believed that a foreign guest had come to pay a visit to his wife at home. So, Mosesy went to see and greet the guest who had come to the house. As he got near to the house he heard someone speaking French, not with a French accent but with a Malagasy accent. When Mosesy got close to the house, Jesus quickly removed the board hanging on the wall. When he came into the house Mosesy didn't see anyone there other than Nenilava. Mosesy asked her who she'd been speaking with, but she didn't answer him; she only laughed. Mosesy returned to his work in the coffee field, but as he left he said, "Are you going crazy, for who else holds a conversation alone with herself?"

It wasn't possible to use the board in the house anymore since Mosesy continued to work not far away. For that reason, Jesus used a book to teach her. Jesus had a large book in which he wrote the words that he was teaching her. The white pages of the book were very, very thin, and the writing was also white. Nenilava had to kneel down and lean in very, very close in order to make out and read the white writings in the book. Even if Mosesy Tsirefo happened to come into the house, he didn't know that Nenilava was studying but thought she was just praying. Jesus also spoke directly into her ears when teaching her, so Mosesy had no idea at all that he was teaching her.

Jesus gave lessons to Nenilava in the house like that for only two days. It was difficult to work at the house, as she was often interrupted by people who came to visit her. For that reason, Jesus relocated the class to the forest. He brought back the board and hung it on a tree and there Jesus gave his instruction. The lessons began at eight o'clock in the morning and finished at eleven each day. Jesus taught her in this way for three days in the forest. During these three days, there were many people in the surrounding area who heard her voice in the woods as she was studying and were afraid, as they thought she had lost her mind. This is why all those who met her on the road wanted to run away. Her parents, too, were disheartened, because they thought that the madness of their child was increasing.

After that Jesus taught her again at home. The time for instruction started each evening at eight o'clock. He first waited for everyone to go to sleep so that they would not interrupt his teaching. This instruction in tongues lasted altogether for three months. She learned twelve great national languages of the world. When she spoke in tongues, she used these twelve languages. Each time she spoke, she used one of these languages, speaking a sentence in one, then moving on to a sentence in another language, and so on, until she had used all twelve languages.

It was in tongues that Nenilava spoke to Jesus, according to what is written: "For one who speaks in a tongue speaks not to humans but to God; for no one understands Him, but he utters mysteries in the Spirit" (1 Cor 14:2).

ii. The Study of the Holy Scriptures

Jesus often coaxed Nenilava to work for him, but she refused over and over again because of her inability to read, write, or preach. Jesus pressed her, however, even though she tried to refuse. Finally she agreed but she also bargained with Jesus. She said to Jesus that if he didn't teach those things she hadn't mastered that were necessary for the work, she couldn't possibly do it. Jesus agreed to teach her, especially the study of the Holy Scriptures. He taught her in heaven; seven times she was transported up to heaven for these lessons.

The way it happened was like this. It was on a Friday that she was first raised up to heaven. When she was raised up, Jesus told her that she would die on Friday at eleven o'clock in the morning. All of the Christians in the district were notified of what was to happen. All those who were able to come arrived at the appointed time. The congregations that couldn't come still sent representatives. A great many people assembled for the occasion. Pastor Rajaona Salema was one of those present for this great event, but Pastor Emmanuel was not free to come.

The service of prayer by the Christians who had gathered was zealous indeed and carried on until the moment came when she was to be taken up to heaven. Nenilava was lying on a bed awaiting the time Jesus had told her. The bed was covered with a clean white sheet, and she asked that another clean white sheet cover her from the chest down, letting her face show. When the time came for her departure, she left gently. All the people who were gathered around her bed held a continuous prayer service through day and night for three days until her return. Discouraged, her parents thought that she would not ever come back. The majority of the Christians present fasted until her return.

The three days passed, and she returned on Sunday at eight o'clock in the morning. When she awoke on the bed, she rose up and preached the word of God in 1 Corinthians 15:55, which says, "O death, where is your victory? O death, where is your sting?" After Nenilava preached, hymn #178 was sung,[3] which goes like this:

1. No one can get to heaven
   If not transported there;
   The one who fights the good fight
   Will persevere and receive the prize.
   Tight and narrow is the door,
   Small and tough is the path that leads there.
   But do not be discouraged, O my friend.
   Those who are unwilling will surely be lost.

---

3. This is the number in the old Lutheran hymnal, *Tiona sy Fihirana*. In Madagascar's current ecumenical hymnal, *Fihirana F.F.P.M.*, it's #377.

2. Many will try to make you stumble,
   But continue in the faith, O my friend.
   Mightily defeat your enemies,
   For they are shrewd and cunning.
   All those sweet things of the world,
   Give them up, for they will betray you.
   May Jesus only be your joy.
   Yes, may you truly rejoice!

3. You shall not receive a crown
   If you do not seek after it.
   But consider your joy
   Once you've come to the beautiful other shore.
   For you shall see the Lord with your own eyes,
   And rejoice in your God.
   So, prepare yourself, O my friend,
   That you may be happy on the Day of Judgment!

4. Oh! You shall not see that good land,
   This is surely true,
   And you will not reach heaven
   If this world is just too sweet for you.
   If you do not trust the Lord,
   Then the fires of hell will be your portion.
   Return, then, for your Redeemer
   Is truly prepared to receive you!

5. So we beg you, we ask you,
   Come home, O wanderer,
   For your Lord wants to receive you right now!
   He doesn't want you to be lost.
   He opens his arms wide to you.
   Offer to him your broken heart.
   Jesus will give you a new and good heart.
   Think on these things, O my friend!

When the many Christians saw and heard this, they repented and wept for joy.

The holy Scriptures that Jesus taught her up in heaven were the four Gospels. Jesus' method of teaching was to use a big ruled wooden tablet of about fifty centimeters long and fifteen centimeters wide. The biggest problem for Nenilava was in distinguishing between chapter and verse in the holy Scriptures. This was due to the fact that she wasn't very good at reading and wasn't at all used to it.

Jesus explained to her first of all what a chapter and a verse were. Then Jesus wrote on the lined wooden tablet the chapter and verse he was teaching her. Jesus then gave her their basic or root meaning. The explanation of the Word was like that given to the two disciples on the road to Emmaus in Luke 24:27, 32: "And beginning with Moses and all the Prophets, he interpreted to them in all the Scriptures the things concerning himself." Then, once their eyes were opened, the two disciples said to one another, "Did not our hearts burn within us while he talked to us on the road, while he opened to us the Scriptures?"

Such is the story of her being lifted up and of the teaching given to her in heaven. She wasn't someone who agreed with everything she was told. She asked Jesus every time for the meaning of the holy Scriptures that were not clear to her.

All those who have heard her preach are in agreement that it was really Jesus who had taught her, for it was truly amazing how she opened up the true meaning of the holy Scriptures on which she preached.

All preachers take a lot of time to prepare before they can feel confident in preaching before the public. Nenilava, on the other hand, could deliver in one day many sermons that everyone was captivated by and that always pierced the hearts of those who heard her preach.

The reason all this was possible was not due to her great abilities at all but because of Jesus, who taught her and always stood by her side and revealed to her what she should say to those who listened to her.

V. The Battle with the Beast

Jesus told Nenilava that she would have to do battle against the beast, which is called the dragon. The reason for making her combat the beast was to teach her to fight, because the struggles she was to face would be very tough indeed. If she could defeat the beast, she could then also triumph over all the other difficult struggles that were before her. But if she didn't triumph, she would not be victorious in all the other struggles to come and would not complete the work she was called to do, because the work she was to do was to be very difficult indeed.

Nenilava's combat with the beast lasted for three days of continuous struggle. Jesus, who was always by her side, taught her how to fight. Jesus carried her to a little forest called Bevorotsiky to fight the dragon. It was nine o'clock in the morning when the battle against the beast began. Before the fight against the beast commenced, Jesus laid his hands on her to give her strength. After he had done so, Jesus said to her, "Be not afraid, for I am your strength. From this moment on, you will defeat him." Jesus told Nenilava, when fighting against the beast, to kneel and not to stand.

The face of this dragon resembled that of a crocodile but with a mane. Spikes measuring about ten centimeters covered its body. She and it fought like people rolling on the floor, body to body, with her chest up against the spiny chest of the beast. Her body was flattened against that of the beast and its spikes pierced Nenilava's flesh. Even more, its paws in front and back grabbed her and its pointed claws penetrated into Nenilava's body. Among other things it used its tail, which looked like the tail of a crocodile, to smack the ground and strike Nenilava vigorously.

The beast tried by every means to make Nenilava fall to the ground, but her kneeling posture, as Jesus had said, prevented the beast from doing it. When Jesus saw that she was at the point of collapsing, he separated them so that she could have a little respite for ten minutes. When the ten minutes had passed, the combat resumed.

Four times a day, Nenilava struggled against the beast. When the struggle was over, Jesus took Nenilava back to her home. For three days in a row this appalling struggle went on. Nenilava's body was covered with wounds and bruises. Jesus passed his hand over her body, however, and immediately she was healed.

On the third day of combat with the beast, Nenilava triumphed over the beast in the name of Jesus, and the beast ran away. Nenilava then found herself totally exhausted. She could not even remember if she was seated or walking. The reason for this state of near-unconsciousness was because of the draining nature of the struggle she had been engaged in; her mind, her thoughts, as well as her whole body were all utterly exhausted. This state of general fatigue continued for a whole month.

Nenilava did not eat for two and a half months. In place of normal food, she was given something round and white to eat. It was something like communion bread. It was, however, only about a seventh the size of a communion wafer. Five of these breads would sustain her for a whole week. She recalls that she felt truly full after eating these little breads. Here's the really amazing thing about it: she remembers feeling very strong after eating this bread, more so than after eating normal food. She fasted in this way for nine years. During this time Jesus did not permit her to eat rice, though she could eat bread, manioc, sweet potatoes, and taro root. She didn't eat all these things together, but varied her consumption of them. She never ate enough to make her full, because Jesus set a limit on how much she could eat.

Nenilava would finish her meal with a cup of a kind of green tea from the *anamamy* plant.[4] She was not given anything that would have strengthened her body, and that was why she wasn't given any rice, because that was the staple of the Malagasy diet. During this time of fasting, Nenilava hardly spoke to anyone. And, if she spoke, it was in tongues. According to her, Jesus asked her not to eat before any great work that he wanted her to do. This fasting was one of the ways of preparing her for the great work that she came to do.

VI. Signs and Wonders

The Lord Jesus often works through signs and wonders. Jesus causes those who follow him sometimes also to perform signs in order to sanctify the word that they preach (cf. Acts 14:3–17). These signs are timeless tools in the hands of God, which he assigns to all who believe in him to do without distinction and in all times and seasons (Mark 16:17–18). Nenilava performed many signs in her work in every place she went. These signs will be told of in this next section of the story. The region of Antsirabe was where she first began her work, except for that which she did in the District of Manakara, where she is from. So, we pick up our story of her work in Antsirabe.

The Spiritual Work in Antsirabe

Antsirabe is the headquarters of the Norwegian Lutheran Mission in Madagascar. It was there also that became the center of where Nenilava worked after she left Vohipeno-Manakara, the district from which she came. It was

---

4. A member of the nightshade family, probably either *Solanum nodiflorum* or *Solanum nigrum*.

in the home of retired pastor Rajosefa Danielson where she and her coworkers stayed when they first came to Antsirabe. This wasn't simply where they stayed, but also where they first began their spiritual work. The first Sunday after they came there is where she first preached in Antsirabe. The people were amazed when they saw her preaching in traditional dress! If we think about this from a human point of view, you would think that it would be embarrassing to appear in front of a bunch of sophisticated people in traditional clothing which was not at all in the fashion of modern times! That was not, however, the first or most important thing of urgency to the Lord. Instead it was the revealing of his word to the people. It was that mission that compelled Nenilava in her work and continued to do so.

The Monday after that first Sunday in Antsirabe, Nenilava began her spiritual work in the home of Baba ("Papa") Rajosefa. One evening they were talking together in the house. What they were discussing together was the question that Baba Rajosefa had asked Nenilava concerning exactly how Jesus appeared to her. While she was sharing her story, one person began to oppose what she was saying and expressed a lack of belief in the whole of her work. When Jesus saw this, he said to Nenilava, "Enough of this; say no more, because this person will *never* believe you." Despite what Jesus had said, Nenilava continued to speak, and so Jesus again spoke to her, saying, "Hey, are you being stubborn and not doing what I told you?" So Jesus swatted her and she fainted and remained unconscious for about a half hour. When she regained consciousness, she realized that she had been disobedient to the Lord, and because of that she repented before the Lord.

The next day many people affected by diverse illnesses were brought to Nenilava so that, once again, she undertook to work with her friends. Among the persons coming to her were the mentally ill, paralytics, epileptics, the needy, and all who were looking to Jesus to deliver them from evil.

Many among these people were healed by Jesus, thanks to his power. From this moment, an important number of the population of Antsirabe began to believe. People coming from the capital, Antananarivo, also came to attend these gatherings of prayer and healing.

A man who had come from Antananarivo attended a gathering one day, but Jesus refused to let anyone lay hands upon him. Nenilava then asked Jesus the reason why they shouldn't lay hands upon this man. He answered her, "For the strongest of reasons it is strictly forbidden for you to lay hands upon him." For three days running this man implored Jesus for healing, but it was not granted. So he just went home.

Everyone had his or her own complaints to bring to Jesus at that time. One person came to complain of problems in his household. Another came to complain about the stubbornness of her children. Jesus gave a suitable word to proclaim to each of these persons, a word that was delivered with a view toward true contrition and repentance in everyone, even if the majority of those coming for healing were Christians.

It was not only in Antsirabe, but everywhere and every time Nenilava preached the word of God Jesus gave her the word or biblical verse that she should speak to the person involved. When she had finished preaching, the Holy Spirit would descend and the hearers would be pierced by the word; everyone would weep and acknowledge their sins before Jesus. Then the rite of casting out demons would begin, for many demons were present. The demons were cast out, the mentally ill regained their senses, and the sick were healed, thanks to their faith in Jesus. The laying-on of hands was then provided for all the people who had gathered, with no exceptions.

Nenilava worked like this for a month in Baba Rajosefa's home. His large house contained many rooms, four of which were always filled with people. Four pastors worked there alongside Nenilava in their spiritual work in that place.

One day, a very agitated person with a demon arrived, led by his mother. This man had a demon cast out of him in the south room of the house. The demon in the man caused him to shake uncontrollably and then caused him to leave the house and go out into the yard. Everyone was afraid of him and so they ran away. This caused a great uproar and many cried out. Nenilava, who was upstairs, heard the commotion. She came down to see and recognized the demon-possessed man holding in his hands an axe and challenging the people: "If any man comes toward me, I will cut off his head!" Because of this, no one dared come near him. Nenilava approached the man and said, "In the name of Jesus, I command you to set down the axe. It is Jesus who commands this of you!" The man did so, placing the axe gently on the ground. Nenilava then picked up the axe and led the man back into the house. Once back in the house, the man was prayed for by Nenilava and then she laid hands on him. He was healed and regained his proper self.

Afterwards, Nenilava questioned him, "Do you remember Jesus?" "Yes," he said. "Then why have you done such a thing?" she asked him. "It was an idea that the devil put into my mind, not my own thoughts," he explained. Nenilava then said, "From now on, believe truly in Jesus and your illness will not return; be strong and pray." After his session with Nenilava on that day, he and his mother returned to their home.

After a month passed, Nenilava continued her work in a church in Antsirabe. She worked for another month in the church. From the beginning of this healing tour, many people came each day from Antananarivo to attend the prayer services and the spiritual work being done there. Nenilava's method of work was quite simple: the word of God was her only tool and it was a powerful tool in her hands. This reliance on the word is what she testified to and preached to the people because it alone has the power to touch people's hearts and make them aware that they are but poor sinners.

Once people came to this awareness of themselves, Nenilava encouraged them to come to Jesus, to hand over to him all their problems and anything not right in their lives. The result of doing this ended in true repentance. When people came to an awareness of their true selves in Jesus, the devil in them had to be sent out.

This issue of casting out demons disturbed many people, giving rise to lots of questions and discussions. Casting out demons, however, is not a new thing; it has existed and has been practiced since the time of Jesus. When Jesus was about to ascend into heaven, one of the things he commanded his disciples to do was to cast out demons (cf. Mark 16:15–18). And in Matthew 10:8 we see that Jesus sent the twelve disciples out on a mission and exhorted them to cast out demons. The devil does not rest. Night and day he is always at work as long as he is still able to capture and afflict people. It is for this reason that we must cast him out of people. This is not done for the honor or glory of the one doing the spiritual work, but to set free those who are bound.

Who were these demon-possessed persons who needed to have their demons cast out? And, who is it that should cast them out?

These questions unfolded from divergent points of view on this question. Some people think that all unbelievers are demon-possessed and so that demon or demons must be cast out. Others say that Christians no longer have demons, so they should not be subjected to exorcism. In writing this book, I have sought only to tell the story of Nenilava and the revival. Its goal is not to offer teaching on this matter or to convince anyone of anything. Nevertheless, it is hard to agree either that all non-believers have demons or that no Christian could ever find him or herself with a demon!

Surely, if a person is a true Christian, then no demon could dwell in him or her. If one is a Christian in name only, however, then one could have a demon in him or her. Already many demons have been cast out of Christians like that. Some of these people were also communicant members of the church.

Who, exactly, is it that should cast out demons? There is no single group of people who should do this kind of spiritual work. Jesus' pronouncement in Mark 16:17 is quite clear: "And these signs will accompany those who believe: in my name they will cast out demons." However, casting out demons is not at all easy, for it implies combat with evil spirits. This necessitates an unshakable faith and complete unity with Jesus, for, according to his own Word, "apart from me, you can do nothing" (John 15:5b).

In doing her spiritual work, Nenilava always followed the preaching of the word of God with the casting out of demons; for, if demons remained in the hearts of the people, they would block them from giving themselves to God and receiving his grace. Once the demons were cast out, then the laying-on of hands was provided for all those who desired it. This is called *fampaherezana* (the act of strengthening), for from it came a power that each person could benefit from if she or he had trust and believed in Jesus. Thus, by the *fampaherezana*, many sick people of all kinds were healed.

Because of the spiritual work that was done at Antsirabe, many sick were healed: the lame walked and the deaf heard. Jesus truly manifested his glory in this great place. Jesus' intention, however, was the creation of faith and repentance.

During all the time that they worked in Antsirabe, this was their method. They began their meetings at nine o'clock in the morning and finished at seven in the evening. There was time then for everyone to eat. After their meals, they started over again at eight o'clock and didn't finish until three in the morning. Only then did they eat the meal they would normally have eaten at night. This was their custom during the whole month.

One day, a Thursday, three men made an appearance before Nenilava, namely Rainisoalambo, Rajaofera, and Rakotozandry.[5] They appeared in the church because they had come to visit the gathered assembly. Only Nenilava could see them; no one else could.

That day, the church was full to overflowing. A woman named Razanamalala, a latecomer to the meeting, entered and made her way through the crowd to find herself up in front. Her entrance coincided with the arrival of the three colleagues who were also headed up front, so she knocked

---

5. These three were the founders of, respectively, the Soatanana revival, the Monolotrony revival, and the Farihimena revival—all long since deceased by Nenilava's time!

into the shoulder of Rakotozandry. Razanamalala didn't see anything, but Nenilava did. Bumping into the lady in this way, Rakotozandry looked upon her with love and looked very happy!

On that blessed day, Nenilava told the assembly about how the three colleagues had joined them and she went on to describe them to the people. She said that Rainisoalambo was in trousers and had draped himself in a traditional *lamba*,[6] and he wore a big hat. Rajaofera had on a long white garment resembling a pastor's robe and carried in his hand a trumpet. Rakotozandry also wore a pastor's robe but carried a big book in which he said were found the names of all people.

Then Rajaofera said to Nenilava, "Approach, and we will explain to you the reason for our coming here." Rajaofera continued,

> We have come to strengthen you, for the mission that will be assigned to you will be very difficult. You have been called to bring spiritually dead Christians to life! You will also have the task to call unbelievers to Jesus, for the day of judgment is coming, that all might repent and leave behind those sins to which they have become accustomed, for the Lord will arrive at an unexpected time. You must work hard and do all that you can in the years allowed to you, in favorable conditions and in unfavorable ones, for the trumpet will sound on that day, so that even the dead will hear the voice of Jesus.

Rakotozandry added, "The book will be opened—the book of life, in which are featured the names of all people. When the time comes, there will be read there the portion assigned to each, according to what he or she has done." After having said this, the three colleagues departed and were seen no more.

Nenilava then lost consciousness and didn't know what was going on. Then Jesus came and said to her, "They have left now, so you should get to work." After she heard this, Nenilava awoke and explained to the people what had just transpired. Everyone then wept for joy and repented, because they knew the truth about themselves.

When they had finished their spiritual work at the church, they had some time for sharing and giving a chapter and verse from the holy Scriptures to each person there. These portions of the holy Scriptures were all from Jesus and meant for each individual person. In every place where Nenilava visited, she always shared a special Scripture for all in this way.

---

6. A traditional Malagasy cloth often used as a shawl.

Some time later, Nenilava asked Jesus if they could stop sharing out special Scriptures for each person. She had two reasons for making this request of the Lord. She thought that too much time was lost in searching the Scriptures for just the right verse for each person, which could better be used in their other work. Also, people wouldn't keep their special Scripture that they were given; they'd lose them and then come back asking for another! So more time was lost in searching for their special Scripture that had been recorded in a notebook. Her other reason for asking for a change was that a certain group called the Mandoa (literally, the Vomiters) were imitating her practice of giving Scripture verses to each person. They came around asking for copies of the notebooks in which were written down the verses given to each Christian in the churches of Ambatovinaky in Antananarivo. The Mandoa sect wanted to use these same verses.

A great revival was the fruit of this divine work in the city of Antsirabe and its environs through God's servant, Nenilava. Many Christians whose hearts had become cold became brave and zealous again, and many who were non-believers were converted and were added to those who belong to the Lord.

The Spiritual Work at Antanamanjaka

When their spiritual work in Antsirabe was done, Nenilava and her coworkers took up their work in Antanamanjaka. As was their custom, the word of God was the foundation of their work. When Nenilava got to this town she began to preach the word of God. Right in the middle of Nenilava's preaching, a person there began to shake violently. Nenilava was obliged to interrupt her preaching on account of the powerful shaking of this person and to cast out the demon from the person in the name of Jesus. During the act of casting the demon out, this person began to speak and cry out very loudly, without anyone understanding the words that were spoken. Finally, the demon came out and the person recovered his senses and sat down. Apart from this person, many other demons also appeared, so they were also cast out of the people who had them. In the name of Jesus, she commanded all the evil spirits to leave. The church itself trembled, for the Holy Spirit had come down upon that place!

At this time, there was a woman named Angeline who was possessed by a powerful demon. She continually cried out until her tongue ended up hanging far out of her mouth! So Jesus said to Nenilava, "Restrain her from speaking, for she is full of evil charms which come forth from her tongue, her head, her forehead, underneath her lips, her forearms, and her palms." This was so because the woman had long served the devil as her master.

If not for Jesus, no one would have been able to heal her because she had made a pact with the devil. After this woman had been healed, Nenilava prayed again for all those gathered there. All those present who had witnessed this wonder wept greatly because of their repentance and gave their lives totally over to Jesus.

At that time, there was also a doctor who had come from Antananarivo. He sincerely repented and knelt down before Nenilava, saying, "Nenilava, does Jesus know me?" She responded, "Yes, he knows you. He called you when you were still a child." Dr. Ramasitera was the name of that person.

The laying-on of hands began at eleven o'clock in the morning for the many people in the church and finished up at ten in the evening. Pastor Rakotosalama and Razanamalala assisted Nenilava with the laying-on of hands at that time. After the *asa* (spiritual work) was done at night, many went back to their homes, but many people chose to stay and sleep at the church for fear of not having a place at the prayer meeting which began again early, at three o'clock in the morning!

When morning came, Jesus spoke with Nenilava and told her about the scar marring the church. He told her of all the different fights that the church had had with the pastor, because of the things that he had done. Jesus instructed Nenilava to call the pastor to meet with her. The meeting took place in the home of the catechist, Rakotomanana. Nenilava spoke first in tongues before revealing all to the pastor. After having heard it all, the pastor admitted everything with his lips, but in his heart he denied it all.

Jesus spoke again to Nenilava and said, "Ask the pastor and the church to offer each other mutual forgiveness of their sins." The two parties met, but the church hesitated to offer their forgiveness because the pastor did not really acknowledge his sins. Because of the unwillingness of the church to forgive, Jesus struck Nenilava and she fainted. She remained unconscious from eight o'clock in the morning until ten at night.

When Nenilava regained consciousness she called Ravaoarisoa, who is called Mamavao, and asked her why she wasn't present at the meeting for mutual forgiveness. Ravaoarisoa explained that she had been prevented from attending because she was caring for someone who was sick.

Then they entered together into the church and undertook to reconcile the parishioners and the pastor by offering each other forgiveness. When everyone was present, Jesus commanded Nenilava to say to the church, "Behold, I, Jesus, have set this pastor before you; whoever has something to complain of against him, let him forgive so that he may receive forgiveness in turn." The church accepted this mutual forgiveness except for five men who turned their backs on the pastor and refused to forgive him his sins. The pastor repented of his sins before Jesus and announced that he would no longer do those things that had nearly destroyed his pastoral vocation. After the mutual repentance, Nenilava began to preach. The Holy Spirit fell upon the church and persuaded many people to accept Jesus. Then demons were cast out and the laying-on of hands concluded the meeting.

God accomplished great works in Antanamanjaka, and his glory was shown forth there. The word of God in 2 Peter 3:9 was fulfilled: "The Lord is not slow to fulfill his promise as some count slowness, but is patient toward you, not wishing that any should perish, but that all should reach repentance."

The Spiritual Work at Loharano

When the spiritual work was done at Antanamanjaka, Nenilava returned again to Anranovisy. From there, the missionaries brought her and her coworkers to Loharano.

After coming there, the visitors went directly to the church, as was their custom, to preach the word of God. After the sermon, many people repented, but also many demons became active. Seeing this, a missionary named Borgenvik asked Nenilava, "Why do you make people vomit?" Nenilava responded, saying, "It isn't me who makes them vomit, but the devil who does it!" Despite her explanation, the missionary did not believe it. After casting out the demons from the people there, they all returned to their right minds. After that the laying-on of hands was provided for the many people who were gathered there.

Once the meeting was over, everyone went home. The missionary and his wife, however, accompanied Nenilava to where she was staying and asked her many questions about her relationship with Jesus. These are some of the questions they asked her: "How is it that you manage to speak directly with Jesus? Do you see him with your own eyes, or do you only hear his voice?" "I see him," Nenilava said. Their questions to her continued: "Why doesn't Jesus manifest himself to us *vazaha*[7] but only

---

7. *Vazaha* literally means "foreigner" and is used for all persons who are not Malagasy.

to you?" "I have no response to that; ask Jesus yourself, for only he can answer you." Then Jesus gave Nenilava the word in John 16:5–9 for the missionaries: "But now I am going to him who sent me, and none of you asks me, 'Where are you going?' But because I have said these things to you, sorrow has filled your heart. Nevertheless, I tell you the truth: it is to your advantage that I go away, for if I do not go away, the Helper will not come to you. But if I go, I will send him to you. And when he comes, he will convict the world concerning sin and righteousness and judgment: concerning sin, because they do not believe in me."

After reading these verses, Nenilava began to explain them. When she was finished, the missionary asked her another question, "Why does Jesus choose to manifest himself to some people but not to others?" When Jesus saw that he was asking such an odd question, he said to Nenilava, "I will make you faint, in order to get him to leave you." So Nenilava fainted, and the missionary was concerned and was filled with fear: "It's because of me that this has happened!" Seeing what had occurred, the missionary's wife wept and said, "Aren't you afraid because of what has happened here? It is all because of *you*!" The missionary responded, saying, "I had to do what I thought was right in order to discern the truth about all of this, but what has happened is my fault. I therefore will repent before Jesus."

The couple did not leave the place where Nenilava was until she had regained consciousness, all the while praying to Jesus to restore her to life. After about an hour, Nenilava regained consciousness.

Then the couple rejoiced and the wife embraced Nenilava, while her husband shook her hand, saying, "From now on I will accept that fact that it really is Jesus who speaks to you." After that, the evening proceeded with a worship service, and then the missionary couple returned to their home. These works and the things that took place at Loharano remind us of the words of Jesus in Matthew 11:25–26, which say, "I thank you, Father, Lord of heaven and earth, that you have hidden these things from the wise and understanding and revealed them to little children; yes, Father, for such was your gracious will." Yes, all the wise and the intelligent must abase themselves before God's divine will. And the apostle Paul says, "But who are you, O man, to answer back to God? Will what is molded say to its molder, 'Why have you made me like this?'" (Rom 9:20).

Coastal Malagsy, however, who are predominantly of African heritage, will usually refer to the Merina, who are pure Melanesians in ancestry, also as *vazaha*. Both groups, however, are immigrants to the island. The truly indigenous people are called *vazimba*.

Remember, dear readers, "God opposes the proud but gives grace to the humble" (Jas 4:6). "Humble yourselves, therefore, under the mighty hand of God, so that at the proper time he may exalt you" (1 Pet 5:6).

The Spiritual Work at Soanindrariny

After their work was done at Loharano the missionary couple accompanied Nenilava to Soanindrariny. They went to the home of an elder of the church. They came there at nine in the morning and by 10:30 began their spiritual work.

As was her custom, Nenilava immediately began to teach and to preach the word of God, for that was their reason for being in Soanindrariny. The people were touched by the word of God, so that many came to know themselves as sinners and repented. Also, all people who approached received the laying-on of hands and prayers for strengthening. Lastly, the work of casting out demons concluded the worship time.

The missionary continued to be opposed to the casting out of demons because it was something he didn't truly believe in, and above all he was against the idea that Christians could be possessed by demons. He didn't even believe that it was the devil who caused people to froth at the mouth. He said to Nenilava, "It is because you tickle their throats with a feather that these people end up frothing at the mouth and vomiting." As they began their work at Soanindrariny, he reminded Nenilava that she shouldn't tickle people with a feather anymore!

They began to cast out demons and all evil spirits were commanded to leave people in the name of Jesus. Then many demons began to be active and to cause many and various parts of the assembly to vomit. There was a woman who was possessed of a demon who was sitting right beside the missionary Borgenvik. The demon caused her to vomit foam from her mouth so that his pants were stained with vomit. This woman was a Christian.

After that experience, the missionary no longer believed that a bird feather was what caused people to vomit, but that it was the work of the devil and that, even if a person was a Christian, one could still be possessed by a demon. The woman spoken of here was a communicant and also the wife of the catechist. Such possession was because of backsliding and weakness of every kind and the cold-heartedness of many believers. Many believers still had faith in their ancestral charms and idols, and this is what made them cold-hearted.

Many Christians were released from demons at that time. They worked four days in that place and demons were cast out every day.

The fourth day, the local midwife invited Nenilava and her friends to visit her. Around noon, Razanamalala said to Nenilava, "Let's go and eat, for the one who invited us is calling for us to come," that is, the town midwife, an honored personage in every Malagasy town. "We have not finished our spiritual work," responded Nenilava. "Let us finish it first." Razanamalala, however, was adamant: "The hostess is waiting for us! The work we can continue later!" The people were very sad and complained, "Is there some sin we've done that we should not receive the grace that was offered to us?" In hearing this, Nenilava's heart was overwhelmed with sadness; however, she did not feel that she could oppose her colleague for fear of causing her sadness, too.

So they left their work unfinished and went to the midwife's house. Some people followed them to the midwife's home, but they didn't receive what they needed because the food for Nenilava and her coworkers had already been prepared. Afterwards, those in the house recited the Lord's prayer together.

After the prayer was over, Jesus spoke to Nenilava, saying, "You shall not partake of this food, for you have failed to do the work for which you were sent." Nenilava was forbidden to eat for five days and the invited guests also decided not to eat! At that time, Nenilava spoke in tongues because that is how she conversed with Jesus. Since she could not eat, Nenilava left, got into a car, returned to Antsirabe, and stayed again at the house of Rajosefa in Andranovisy.

The story of the spiritual work in Soanindrariny reveals to us that our Jesus is a Jesus who works without carelessness at all times.

One day, in Samaria, when Jesus' disciples wanted him to eat, he told them he would not eat until his work was done. The disciples talked together and then asked, "Has anyone brought him something to eat?" Jesus said to them, "My food is to do the will of him who sent me and to accomplish his work" (John 4:31–34).

When we can also say, "Our work is to do the will of Jesus alone," then Jesus will say to us, "Do not work for the food that perishes, but for the food that endures to eternal life, which the Son of Man will give to you. For on him God the Father has set his seal" (John 6:27).

The Spiritual Work at Masinandraina

Nenilava and her coworkers took a day of rest at Antsirabe after their work at Soanindrariny. Then the group went to the district of Masinandraina again. They stayed at the home of Pastor Rajaobelina when they got to the district. Along the way, Jesus advised Nenilava that twenty-seven men had separated themselves from the district of Masinandraina to found an independent church under the direction of a pastor in the district. "The pastor will present himself to you and your coworkers once you are in the city," Jesus warned her. When they arrived in town, sure enough, this pastor presented himself to them. After a time of prayer in the home of Pastor Rajaobelina, this visiting pastor addressed himself to Nenilava, saying, "Madame, I have come to invite you to stay at my home." Before Nenilava could even respond, Jesus intervened, saying, "You must not go to that house." So Nenilava simply said to the pastor, "I cannot accept your invitation because I have too much work to do here." This refusal of Nenilava's is explained by the fact that Jesus had already told her all about the situation in that district in advance of their coming there. In fact, this pastor wanted to exchange ideas with her about his plot to divide the district and separate them from the missionaries.

This visiting pastor having left, Nenilava explained to Rajaobelina, "The reason this pastor came here was to invite me to stay at his home, but I refused because Jesus warned me that he was trying to cause division, and after two days, he will make his appearance again at Masinandraina."

After two days, he did in fact show up at Masinandraina, but the missionaries didn't know of his plans because he was so two-faced to them. Afterwards, Nenilava and her retinue also arrived in Masinandraina. As was her custom, she began to preach and to cast out demons and laid hands on all those who presented themselves to her. She then gave out Bibles to people and it wasn't until seven in the evening that they left.

Nenilava occupied half the home of the missionary there. When they arrived there, the wife of another missionary came and invited them all to come and eat at her house. When they got to her house, the missionary there asked Nenilava, "What do you think about this district here?" Nenilava said to him, "I know this district very well because the Lord has already told me about it. There will be twenty-seven men who are going to try to split off from this district." So the missionary again asked her, "Is that really what Jesus told you?" Nenilava responded, "It's the truth, for this will happen in a year's time and these people will put their plans into action."

"Well, we'll see about that, but let's pray God that these plans come to nothing," said the missionary. Nenilava said, "The devil is already working in them to bring to fruition his project. Their plan isn't an empty one." The missionary thought to himself, "Has this really come from Jesus and will it really come to be?" His wife, however, believed this word from the beginning. When the meal was over, everyone left.

The next morning, the wife of the missionary came to ask Nenilava about herself, her husband, and their work. After they spoke together they went to the church to begin their work. Their way of working did not vary. Their usual pattern was that they preached the word, cast out demons in Jesus' name, and practiced the work of strengthening for all who came forward for this work.

It was then that the missionary could not keep from remarking that the five garments that Nenilava wore were all thoroughly soaked in sweat as if they had been soaked in water. He then had to admit that this power in her was surely not her own but came from God. After the work of strengthening was completed, everyone went back to their homes. Even though the service was over, individual consultations followed at the dwelling of the missionary for all who came there for it.

On the third day of their work at Masinandrina, a girl of eighteen years, who had a weakness since birth that left her unable to stand up or even to feed herself, came to them. Her parents brought her and her sister to the church. Nenilava and her friends took turns preaching. When the sermon was over, Nenilava approached the girl with weakness in her legs and asked her, in Jesus' name, "Do you know Jesus?" "Yes," the girl replied. Then Nenilava continued her questioning, "How is it that you know Jesus?" The girl said, "I know that Jesus is a prophet and he raises up the weak." Nenilava asked her then, "Do you believe that Jesus can make the lame walk?" "Yes," said the girl. Then many more questions followed. "Who is the weak one whom Jesus will heal today?" She answered, "I am the lame one that Jesus is going to heal today!" "Do you truly believe that Jesus is going to raise you up?" Nenilava asked. "Yes, I truly believe that Jesus will raise me up now!" So Nenilava said to her, "If you believe in Jesus, who raises up the lame, then arise!" She then stood up and began to walk all around the church. All the missionaries were amazed at the faith of this girl and of her healing.

At the end of the meeting, the girl went out and walked all around in the churchyard and everyone saw her. This great work brought the glory of

God to this church. No one any longer had to assist her as she walked home on her own! On the way, she couldn't stop saying, "In the name of Jesus I was raised up, in the name of Jesus I can walk!"

Their work at Masinandriaina was completed, so Nenilava and her companions returned again to Antsirabe. On their way there, two brothers who served idols both died on the same day. They were on their way to sell charms and amulets in Antsirabe. They had rented a car from Razanamalala, and her brother was the one driving the car. By an irony of fate, this very same car had taken Nenilava and her associates to Antsirabe, and they had planned to rent it themselves for their return to Antsirabe, but the driver had already rented the car to the two aforementioned brothers.

Before they had left, Razanamalala had strongly reproached her brother for having rented her vehicle to the two brothers. She even asked the two renters if they would leave the car and find another. But they answered her harshly, saying, "No, we won't give up the car, for it is ours. Didn't we already pay for the rental of it?" Razanamalala couldn't reason with their obstinacy, so she was forced to find another vehicle. She didn't at all like the idea of traveling together with sellers of amulets and charms!

But on the way to Antsirabe an accident occurred. The car that these two dealers in amulets and charms were traveling in collided violently with another car, and the two brothers were both killed. It was good, though, that Nenilava did not utter any harsh words against these two brothers, for she felt that it was God alone who could judge others, as it says in God's word: "Vengeance is mine, I will repay, says the Lord" (Rom 12:19).

At that time, Nenilava was weighed down by a great sadness. Two things in particular saddened her: first, the sudden death of the two brothers, and second, the fact that the car that she had used to go and preach the gospel had also been used to transport charms and fetishes of idols.

The way that these two brothers were killed was like this: the first one had his head torn off completely, while the second one's head was totally crushed. Nenilava was saddened and wept upon seeing the bodies. She also gave one of her own cloths to cover up their broken bodies.

Nenilava stayed for two days in Antsirabe before moving on to Mandrosohasina.

The Spiritual Work at Mandrosohasina and Vinaninkarena

Nenilava and her associates remained for a week while working in Mandrosohasina.[8] Their customary way of work didn't change at all from the way they had worked everywhere before. All they did there was preach God's word and do the spiritual work of strengthening and casting out demons. Many were those hungry for the word of God who followed her to Mandrosohasina. Many of those who came there were from Antananarivo and Mahajanga.[9]

After their spiritual work at Mandrosohasina was done, they returned once again to Antsirabe. From there they went to work in Vinaninkarena. Their work consisted above all in settling disputes between the pastor and the elders of the church. The work of settling these fights lasted three whole days! Once everyone had come to their senses, the two parties completely forgave one another.

The Spiritual Work at Manandona

After their work at Vinaninkarena was done, Nenilava and her coworkers returned to Antsirabe again. After a rest there, they continued on to Manandona. They also worked there for one week. When they got there, a man, the retired chief officer of the canton, approached her. While still back home, however, he had said to his friends, "The reason I'm going to meet with Nenilava is to hear if Jesus really speaks with her or not. And if Jesus knows the thoughts of my heart and can tell me everything that I've ever done, then I will believe in him!"

However, before he got there, Jesus shared with Nenilava all the thoughts and the words spoken by this man. When he came into the front yard of where Nenilava was staying, Jesus said to Nenilava, "Behold, this unbeliever is out in front of the house; I'm going to tell him everything he has ever done." When the man came into the house, he exchanged greetings with Nenilava. Once the traditional greetings were out of the way, Nenilava began to pray. She then preached and spoke to him from the word of God. Then, when their conversation was concluded, she asked him, "What is the purpose of your visit?" He answered, "I have come to

---

8. The literal meaning of Mandrosohasina is "moving toward the holy."

9. The Malagasy text reads "Mojanga," which appears to be a typo or alternate spelling for Mahajanga, a port city on the west coast of Madagascar.

approach Jesus so that he can tell me everything that I've ever done." Nenilava said to him again, "Is that truly your desire, that Jesus tell you everything that you have done?" "Yes," he said, "that is truly what I desire, so that I can ask forgiveness and repent." That was not at all what was in his heart, of course; he just wanted to know if Jesus spoke with Nenilava or not. "If Jesus doesn't really speak with her," he said, "I will try to stop everyone from coming to meet with her ever again!"

However, in front of Pastor Rakotosalama and his coworkers as well as all the other people present in the house, Nenilava began to reveal everything that this man had done. Nenilava said to him, "You listen here now to what Jesus has to say concerning all your ways! When you were the chief officer of the canton, you stole ten zebus and stole two hundred thousand francs. When people paid you money for government identity cards, you told them it wasn't enough to get the job done and made them pay a second time. You even forced some folks to pay two or three times; in this way you stole the people's money." Then Jesus spoke to him through Nenilava, saying, "If you do not gather together all the people to whom you have done wrong and ask their forgiveness, I also will surely not forgive you. But if you do this thing, then I will forgive you." In hearing these words the man was totally staggered, and he said, "I repent before you, Jesus. Forgive me my sins. I shall do as you have said." Jesus answered him, "Go, and do what I have commanded you!" Having not yet received Jesus' forgiveness, he began to sob uncontrollably; he left the house and went back home, full of grief and despair.

Nothing was ever done of what Jesus had commanded him, for not only did the people he had defrauded not live in the same locale as him, but they were scattered in different places all over the canton. Furthermore, his advanced age handicapped him from going to all these areas where he had worked and where so many lived whom he had betrayed. Though he complained bitterly and repeatedly asked for forgiveness, he did not receive it because of his evil character. "Blessed is the one whose transgression is forgiven, whose sin is covered. Blessed is the man against whom the Lord counts no iniquity, and in whose spirit there is no deceit" (Ps 32:1–2).

The Children That People Gave to Nenilava

Jesus had promised Nenilava to give her many children, according to the promise given to her in Isaiah 54:1: "'Sing, O barren one, who did not bear;

break forth into singing and cry aloud, you who have not been in labor! For the children of the desolate one will be more than the children of her who is married,' says the Lord."

This word was literally fulfilled. Indeed, Nenilava had many children from the Lord God. From the farthest southern portion of the island to the farthest north lived her children, all of them children according to the Spirit. God did not only give her spiritual children but also gave her children in the flesh.[10] She now has three children, all boys—apart from the others yet to come—who were given outright to her by their parents.

The First Child

After the work in Manandona was completed, Nenilava and her coworkers returned again to Antsirabe. They stayed the whole while at the home of Rajosefa Danielson. They worked there for four days. Afterwards, they all went back home to Ankaramalaza to remain there for four months.

In the month of March, though, they went up again to Antsirabe and stayed once more at Andranovisy. They arrived there on a Friday. The following Tuesday, a woman named Razaiarivelo came to the house where they were staying. Many other people also came there on that day.

The meeting began with a time of prayer, followed by preaching from the word of God for all the people who had gathered there. All were deeply struck by the word of God, so that everyone cried. After the sermon they began to cast out demons in the name of Jesus and commanded all the evil spirits to depart. After that came the laying-on of hands. Razaiarivelo was the first of many to come forward. She first knelt down before Nenilava and said: "Before you lay hands on me, Neny, I have something to say to you." Then, weeping uncontrollably, she said, "Oh, Neny, I am carrying a child, but I don't know if he is even my child or not, for Jesus has said to me, 'This child is not yours. He belongs to Nenilava. So, when he is born, give him to her.'" Before all of this happened, Jesus had already shown the child to Nenilava in a vision. She had dreamed about giving birth to a plump child with light skin. A year after she had this vision, these things told of her came to be.

When the time came, the child was born. At three weeks old, the baby was brought by his parents to Vohipeno. Then the mother and father went

10. This means that she gained "children according to the Spirit" through her spiritual work as well as adopted children in her personal care "in the flesh."

on to Ankaramalaza to present the child to Nenilava. They handed the child over to Nenilava at a town called Mandrondra. It was also there that he was baptized. The child's name is Germain Rafanomezantsoa Rabearivelo. After the baptism, a photo of the baby was taken on the east side of the church with everyone who was there for the service.

The Second Child

The wife of Pastor Rakotosalama Jaofera had difficulty in conceiving another child. One day, she begged Nenilava to pray for her so that she could have another baby. The couple agreed that if a child should be born to them, they would give the infant to Nenilava. The offering of this child to Nenilava is like the fulfillment of Rajaofera's words from long ago, who once said: "One of my descendants will be sent by God to a land that I do not know. All this will happen later to one of my grandchildren."[11] When he offered up his child, Rakotosalama told of these things. Six months after its birth, the baby was brought to Ankaramalaza; Ramenja, the child's mother, offered him up. It was at the church in Lokomby that she offered the child to Nenilava. When she presented him to Nenilava, this is what she said: "This child has been presented to Nenilava by the Lord; and so I hand him over to her before this congregation." The pastor of this parish, Daniela Ralaivola, was also there, at the presentation of the child to Nenilava. Nenilava took the baby and said, "I thank you all for having given me this child." The name of this second child is called Germain Randrianarijaona Rajaofera.

The Third Child

A woman named Ravaoary had many children. One day, one of her children, named Martin Samoela, became gravely ill with a high fever. When he got sick like that, his mother made plans to bring him to the hospital in Manambaro.[12] Her plans, however, did not work out, and the family was forced to remain where they were.

---

11. The Jaofera spoken of above was an old evangelist and the father of Rakotosalama Jaofera.

12. Manambaro is the location of the Lutheran hospital near Fort Dauphin. From Betroka it is a twelve-hour journey by car. Many Christians, however, made this journey rather than go to government hospitals because people trusted the staff at Manambaro, saying, "They can raise the dead at Manambaro!"

As she thought about the illness of her son and what she could do for him, she heard a voice whisper to her: "It's not this child who is sick, but you, his parents, are the ones who are sick." The couple could not understand the meaning of these words at all at the time. The child's illness grew worse and worse, and so its mother decided to bring him to Ankaramalaza. So she left for there, accompanied by her sister and her five children.

Once there, the seven travelers were shown in to see Nenilava. During their first meeting, Nenilava prayed for them, saying: "It is you, Jesus, who has directed your sisters here to this remote place, so difficult to get to, and where they have never been to before. And so, I ask you to grant them their desires and to give them what they seek from you." After the time of prayer, they explained to Nenilava why they had come, saying, "We have come to bring this sick child here because he is ill." When Nenilava heard this, she said, "I wish to say to you clearly: we don't have any medicine or pills here to give to you to heal this sick child. It is your prayers and your repentance that shall be the medicine to heal your child!"

The two sisters were conscious of their sins, and so they repented, and then the child was healed and made totally well. When the child was well, the family made plans for going home. As they were preparing to go, Ravaoary heard a voice say to her, "Leave the child here in Ankaramalaza to live with the servant of God." Ravaoary responded, however, by saying, "Please leave the child with me; it isn't healthy and it is truly close to my heart; but, if I give birth again, later on, I shall give the child to you gladly." All of them returned home to Betroka, for the child was completely cured.

Later, when Ravaoary had given birth to a daughter, she waited for the voice of Jesus telling her to present this child to Nenilava, according to the promise that she had made in Ankaramalaza. But she heard no such voice, and so she just waited to hear the voice again.

Later Ravaoary gave birth again and bore a son. Thirteen days after its birth, the mother came down with a high fever. The whole family was greatly dismayed because of the nature of her illness. In the course of this great illness the voice came back to her and said, "Offer to Nenilava this child to whom you have just given birth." She did not hesitate for a moment to offer the newborn child to Nenilava, because she had been prepared to do so ever since she made that promise in Ankaramalaza. She spoke with her husband about her plan to offer this child to Nenilava according to the word of Jesus. Her husband did not hesitate either when he heard this but simply said, "This will be a blessing for us if our son becomes a servant of God!" After that conversation, Ravaoary was completely healed of her fever.

As Nenilava passed through Betroka, during her second trip from Ankaramalaza to Fort Dauphin, she met Ravaoary, who said to her, "I have given birth to a boy, dear Neny, and it will be you who will hold the child at his baptism, for from now on he belongs to you." Nenilava said to her, "Yes, I thank you, for even before the child was conceived in your womb, Jesus gave him to me in a vision."

As agreed, the parents were to wait for the return of Nenilava to have the child baptized and to give him over to his adoptive mother. But the mission work of Nenilava in Fort Dauphin lasted longer than expected before she set out to return to Ankaramalaza. At the end of three months of waiting, they could wait no more and made the decision to baptize the child; however, they would await the return of Nenilava to Betroka and then give her the child. It was two months after the baptism before Nenilava arrived back in Betroka and the parents gave her the child. The child was fully seven months old when he was given to Nenilava.

The name of this third child was Merlin Germain Ramanantsoa. The names of his father and mother were Gabriel Randriatavy and Ravaoary Razafindratompo, who resided in Betroka.

The Spiritual Work in Imerina

The spiritual work in Vakinankaratra having finished, Nenilava continued her spiritual work again in the region of Imerina. She made Antananarivo her headquarters. From there she went to many different locations, which will be told about in what follows.

As early as 1953 the people in Antananarivo had invited her to come and visit them. It wasn't until 1954, however, that she was able to get there. She commenced her work there on March 25 and worked there until April 17, 1954.[13]

Nenilava set herself up for work at Ambatovinaky. The program of Jesus for all of Imerina at that time, according to Nenilava, was as it is said in Luke 4:38–44:

> And he arose and left the synagogue and entered Simon's house.
> Now Simon's mother-in-law was ill with a high fever, and they

---

13. Cf. *Ny Mpamangy* (June 1954). *Ny Mpamangy* means "The Visitor." This is the official magazine of the Malagasy Lutheran Church.

> appealed to him on her behalf. And he stood over her and rebuked the fever, and it left her, and immediately she rose and began to serve them. Now when the sun was setting, all those who had any who were sick with various diseases brought them to him, and he laid his hands on every one of them and healed them. And demons also came out of many, crying, "You are the Son of God!" But he rebuked them and would not allow them to speak, because they knew that he was the Christ. And when it was day, he departed and went into a desolate place. And the people sought him and came to him, and would have kept him from leaving them, but he said to them, "I must preach the good news of the kingdom of God to the other towns as well; for I was sent for this purpose." And he was preaching in the synagogues of Judea.

Nenilava's method of working there was the same as she had worked in all the other places to which she had gone. Her preaching did not vary and was always full of power so that she touched the hearts of all who heard her. After the preaching, demons were cast out; then words of strengthening were delivered, followed by the laying-on of hands. Each session of spiritual work ended with the distribution of selections of hymns, and Scriptures were given by Jesus to everyone without charge.

Crowds of people came to each meeting, including both *vazaha* and Malagasy. A great many of them received healing. Many who came were simply the curious, but among them too were those who received the gift of healing, for Nenilava brought them into the presence of Jesus in prayer, saying, "Your brothers and sisters have come here out of curiosity, dear Jesus! So, I ask you to come into their hearts, for they are truly poor in Spirit!"

Everyone received their share of grace from this visit: government leaders, local students, and those who had studied abroad. It was no less so for the mass of the common people.

After the spiritual work in Antananarivo and its environs was completed, Nenilava went to do her work in other cities beyond Imerina.

The Spiritual Work in Ambatovinaky

When Nenilava worked in Ambatovinaky, she preached the word as was her custom. All the sick came to her: the lame, the mute, the mentally ill, the blind, and the deaf. All received healing from Jesus. The lame rose up together, the mute all spoke together, the blind recovered their sight, the deaf heard, and the mentally ill were all healed.

There was a little girl who could walk after having been especially held up in prayer. All the people were amazed to see the power and the mercy of Jesus, which the mind could hardly take in, yet all these things were done in the twinkling of an eye.

One Sunday, when Nenilava preached, modern speakers were installed in the church at Ambatovinaky, so that all of the population of Antananarivo could hear the word of God.

When the sick heard her preaching, together with those who cared for them, many of them made haste to go to Ambatovinaky. All those who came there were healed, and all the time they worked there the miracles of Jesus did not cease.

The Spiritual Work in Toamasina

Like all the other localities already visited by Nenilava, Toamasina also had a thirst for a visit. When Nenilava and her friends and coworkers came there, many people were shown the will of Jesus, and he received them by their acts of repentance.

The prayer service took place in the church. Once everyone was gathered, Nenilava ascended to the pulpit to preach the word of God. Many were pierced by the word, repented of their sins, and accepted Jesus. Representatives of all nations came: the expats, the Chinese, the Indo-Pakistanis, and the Malagasy. Jesus manifested himself to them all by many acts of healing the sick. The blind, the mute, and the lame were all healed by Jesus according to their needs, and in this way his glory was made manifest. Nenilava worked in Toamasina for a month, working every day.

There are many who asked if they had Jesus in them or not. All of them were given assurance from the holy Scriptures delivered to each one personally. This led them to repent of all things not of Jesus.

There was a young man who told of his stubbornness in coming to Jesus. He came to himself, confessed his sin, and repented; he promised not ever to return again to his former ways. He vowed to work for Jesus, indeed, to be his slave for the rest of his days.

There was also a *karana*[14] who had been sick for twelve years. He approached Nenilava and said, "I am sick and I would like to approach this

14. *Karana* is applied to anyone of Indo-Pakistani origin, whether Indians or

Jesus, Son of God, to whom you pray." Then, he added, "If I am healed of my sickness, how much should I pay you? For I do not want you to work for free. I have already spent a lot of money for consultations and medicines and yet I am not cured. So if this Jesus and God that you pray to can heal me, I will give you money."

The response of Nenilava to this *karana* was simple: "I do not seek anything at all from you, but only this, that you believe in Jesus in your heart that you may be saved and that you serve him for the whole rest of your life. If you do that, it will bring me joy."

The *karana* wouldn't agree not to pay money to Nenilava, and Nenilava refused to accept payment. So in the end the man left without being healed of his illness.

There was also a young French woman who had gotten married. Only a week after her wedding, however, she did not know where her husband was. She approached Nenilava and asked her to pray for her to find out where her husband had gone. So, at her request, Nenilava, Mamavao, Razanamalala, and the young woman began to pray together. As they prayed, Jesus said to Nenilava that the husband of this young woman had taken another young woman with him overseas. On hearing this, the young woman began to weep uncontrollably and went kind of crazy. Jesus consoled her by saying to Nenilava, "Comfort her, for I will give her satisfaction, for I will return her husband into her arms again."

After two months abroad he came back. Nenilava preached the word of God to this young woman to establish a strong faith in her. Then Nenilava put the following question to her, "What do you most want and desire, the salvation of your spirit or your husband by your side?" She said, "That Jesus would hear my request and that I, in turn, will be able to give myself to God." Jesus said to her again, "If you receive the answer to your prayers, will you give me your life, your household, and your husband?" The young woman responded, "Yes."

From that time on, she went to the church frequently to hear the word of God and to build up her faith. She agreed to become a Christian, even though her husband had still not come to church. Many couples who had never registered their marital status agreed to regularize their legal married

---

Pakistani or any other Indian-subcontinent peoples. This implies either a Hindu or a Muslim; however, the vast majority of those called *karana* in Madagascar are Muslims. In the French translation, the text reads "Hindu," but this is unlikely.

status with the government.[15] Students from the regional schools also came to the prayer services, and many of them repented of their sins.

One student had taken his exams three times without ever passing them. But because of the student's good and caring nature, the director of his school let him continue his studies. He was among those who approached Nenilava for advice. She preached to him the word of God and revealed the reason that he had not progressed in his academic skills. Jesus told Nenilava that this student had gone to someone from the Comoros Islands, who gave him a ring that featured the head of a man. This ring was his idol and directed everything that he did. Nenilava preached the word of God to him and explained that only in Jesus is there to be found wisdom and a clear mind. She said to him, "If you believe in Jesus you will get what you need." The young man accepted these words and believed.

When Nenilava saw that he believed the words of Jesus that were meant for him, she took the fetish ring in which he had trusted off of his finger. It was a thing of no worth, bringing only lies and deception and had done nothing for him at all. The young man said to Nenilava, "If you take this ring from me, I must give it back to its owner." But Nenilava didn't agree to this and said to him that he must surrender the ring to her because it was a harmful instrument of the devil; it wasn't a thing to hold on to and cherish, for it would bring him nothing but death. So the young man gave the ring back to Nenilava and said that he would come often to hear the word of God. He truly kept his word and also brought many of his student friends with him. There were forty-five students in his class. Only four of them didn't come with him to services. All repented of their sins. During their next exams, the forty-one who had gone to services all got a passing grade, and the one who returned the ring finished in first place, while the four who had refused to come to services finished in last place and didn't pass.

Dear readers! The Lord our God is the God of all! "Therefore the Lord, the God of Israel, declares: 'I promised that your house and the house of your father should go in and out before me forever,' but now the Lord declares: 'Far be it from me, for those who honor me I will honor, and those who despise me shall be lightly esteemed'" (1 Sam 2:30), and then also, "'Behold, I am laying in Zion a stone of stumbling, and a rock of offense; and whoever believes in him will not be put to shame'" (Rom 9:33).

15. As a former French colony, Madagascar does not recognize church weddings as legal affairs. To become legally married, one must appear before a government official and pay a tax to receive a certificate of marriage. Few people at that time bothered to go to the trouble and expense of either a church wedding or a civil wedding.

The Spiritual Work in Maroantsetra

After the spiritual work in Toamasina was complete, Nenilava then worked in Maroantsetra. When they got there, so many people came that the church proved to be too small to contain all those who had gathered and most had to stand outside. Each family brought their sick, the mute, the deaf, the mentally handicapped, and those suffering from various diseases.

There was at that time a Muslim child who had a hearing problem because its ear lacked a hole. This child was four years old. Its parents brought the child to receive healing from Jesus. For three days, time after time, they went back and forth with the child between their home and the house where Nenilava and her friends were. On the third day, Jesus healed the child, who could then hear well. He opened the child's eyes and called out its name and it heard him fine. The child's parents rejoiced greatly because their child was healed. They then believed in Jesus because Jesus is the true God. They committed themselves, saying, "From now on, our whole family will come to worship and believe in Jesus."

After that, many other Muslims in town, the young and the old, came to worship; and they all found satisfaction in Jesus.

There was also a Chinese child carried in who was paralyzed. When its mother came to see Nenilava, the question was asked, "Ma'am, whom have you come here to see?" The Chinese lady answered, "Jesus." She was asked again, "But what is it you want from Jesus?" "My child is paralyzed," she said. Nenilava continued to ask her, "Is it really Jesus you are looking for? And why have you come to him?" Then she said, "Jesus forgives us our sins, and that is why I have come here. It is because of my sins that my child is paralyzed." Then the word of God was proclaimed to the woman, about how Jesus loved her and all people, because he is the Lord of all peoples.

For a day and a half, this woman carried her child to Nenilava because of her faith in Jesus. At that time, the child was two and a half years old and it just sat in the lap of its mother. Then, from her lap, the child began to stand up and walk, thanks to the faith of this woman and her repentance. From that moment on, this woman and her husband became Christians.

There was also a man who had lost his mind and thrown off all his clothes. He had remained like that for ten years. This man stayed in the same house where Nenilava was. He was quite violent because the devil in him was terribly enraged. But after working with this man, he was healed. Many others who had faith in Jesus were healed as well. Only two sick people were not healed; that was because they didn't believe in Jesus.

One day, many people flocked into the church. Many were deeply touched by the word of God, so that a thousand people agreed to be baptized. It took four Malagasy pastors and one missionary pastor to baptize all of these people. Also, four hundred people who were not yet communicants became catechumens at that time. Three hundred fifty couples whose unions were not officially recognized agreed to get a civil marriage.

For two months they did their spiritual work in that district. After that time the visiting evangelists returned home again.

The Spiritual Work in Mananara

Nenilava and her coworkers came next to Mananara. A huge crowd came to welcome them on arrival there. These large gatherings expressed the people's spiritual thirst and willingness to hear the word of God. The spiritual work in this locale lasted for one week. Many people repented and carried their sick ones to the gatherings. There was even one non-believer who came and was healed of his blindness.

There in Mananara was also an elderly blind woman of sixty-five years. She was married to a Frenchman but they had no children. Her expat husband died and she then inherited everything he owned. Sometime later she was remarried to a *karana*. He, too, died, and she inherited all of his fortune. Sadly, when this poor woman reached the age of sixty years, she became blind. Because of her blindness, people were able to take advantage of her and steal all of her wealth, and she became poor. So she was cared for by the local church. When Nenilava arrived in the town of Mananara, the elderly blind woman said to those around her, "Take me to see Nenilava, for I would like to speak with her."

When she met Nenilava, this is what the woman said: "I come to you, child, because my eyes cannot see. I am poor and afflicted and it saddens me that I have become a burden on others. That is why I now ask you to pray to God to take me from this earth without delay. Indeed, I ask that God take me this very day up to heaven!" After the woman spoke, Nenilava laid hands on her that she might have strength and faith in Jesus. When the woman realized that Nenilava had not prayed for her death, she asked Nenilava to pray like this: "'Take this woman home to you, Lord, for she does not want to remain down here on earth anymore but to be with you, Jesus!' This is what you should pray for and ask the Lord to do for me!"

After this sisterly conversation, the woman went back home, for it was night. During the night, Nenilava continued to pray ardently for her according to her wishes. That night, the woman went to sleep, her days on earth were over, and her heartfelt prayer to Jesus was granted. She went home to heaven.

The next morning all the people around Nenilava were filled with amazement and said, "The words of Jesus in John 14 have been fulfilled: 'Whatever you ask in my name, this I will do.'" Nenilava strengthened the people's hearing of the word by adding, "Whatever we ask in faith will be granted."

Then, that night, they organized the Christian community to come together for a time of prayers for comfort in their sorrow at the death of this woman. Their spiritual work complete, the evangelism visitors left that place.

The Spiritual Work at Soanierana Ivongo

When the spiritual work at Mananara was completed, Nenilava came also to Soanierana Ivongo. When it was evening, a worship service at the church was held and everyone brought their sick ones there. Jesus loved to satisfy the needs of each and every one of those who came to him.

The service followed the same basic form as always. They opened with the preaching of the word of God and the work of spiritual strengthening and the casting out of demons. The word of God and the healing of the sick worked together and touched hearts so deeply that they produced true repentance and faith in God.

There was there a blind young boy of ten years who, though not a Christian, was brought to the house where Nenilava was staying by his grandmother, who was also not a Christian, to seek for his healing. It was in the house where Nenilava was staying that this work for the child was done, not in the church. When they gathered together in the house, the word of God was proclaimed to this honorable elderly woman, even though she knew nothing at all about Jesus her savior. Despite this fact, these visiting evangelists were not discouraged at all but redoubled their prayers to Jesus, asking that he reveal his glory to this unbeliever.

They asked the child, "Do you believe that Jesus is able to heal you?" He answered, "Yes." Then Nenilava said to him, "Pray to Jesus!" So he prayed like this: "O Jesus, save me. Not only do I ask that you open my eyes to see, but that I be saved now and until I take my last breath on earth." Three times he repeated this prayer. Nenilava and her friends were simply amazed. The child asked also that his whole family, all of them non-Christians, and above all his grandmother who had brought him there would be saved as well.

When the prayer meeting was finished, the child asked to go outside into the front yard. Out in the yard, no one was holding his hand, for his eyes could see. All the people who were in the house couldn't believe their eyes when they saw him running and playing ball with the other children. Many people saw this amazing thing that happened and together, with Nenilava and her friends, they all gave glory to God!

It was also in Soanierana Ivongo that there was a male driver who kidnapped a young girl who had been sent by her mother to collect greens out in the fields. He had captured this young girl and took her in his car to Toamasina. Her parents searched frantically for her but could not find her.

After going to Toamasina the chauffeur returned home. When he came to a place called Ampasina he left the little girl there. Because of the deep sadness of the little girl, she cried and prayed, saying, "You, O God, created me, and you also made that young man. You know that this situation is not my will, for he is the one who kidnapped me! And so, if you are the God who created him, please see him and what he has done to me!"

On arriving back in Soanierana Ivongo, this young man found that he was totally paralyzed on one side and couldn't even sit up anymore but only lie on his bed so others had to feed him. When Nenilava arrived there, he too came seeking healing. When he approached Nenilava, Jesus said to her, "This young man has deceived people and kidnapped someone's child. The young girl has not been returned to her parents. That is why I have struck him so that he will return her to her parents."

Nenilava told the young man what Jesus said so that he would come to his senses. He confessed his guilt and that it was a sin that would cause him to be lost if he did not repent. So he repented, and for two days he was contrite in repenting of his sin. Then Nenilava asked him again, "Do you truly believe in Jesus?" "Yes," he said. She further asked him, "Do you also believe that he has forgiven your sins?" "Yes," he said. He then stood up, and as he did so the whole house began to shake. All the people were amazed to see him rise up. They cried to see the mercy God had shown him even though the girl he had kidnapped had not yet been returned to her parents.

"When I am fully healed," he said, "I will seek this little girl again. Then I will ask her forgiveness and I will bring her back to her parents." And he said, "From now on I will no longer sin. I will serve Jesus my whole life long until my days are over." He recalled the grace of Jesus to him. The evangelistic visitors worked at Soanierana Ivongo for a week. Then they went back home.

The Spiritual Work at Brickaville and Anivorano

After their spiritual work at Soanierana Ivongo, Nenilava passed through Toamasina again and worked there for a week. This time they worked primarily among the pupils in the boys' dormitory.

Three pupils snuck out at night. They passed by the house where Nenilava was staying, then went in and listened to the word of God and the teaching going on there. When they heard the word of God they all repented, demons were cast out of them, and hands were laid on them. As they left, they were encouraged to come back for the next meeting and invite their friends along also.

Indeed, at the next meeting, twenty-five pupils came and Jesus was made known to them. There was preaching of the word and they were encouraged not to be disrespectful toward their teachers. All of them, like their friends before them, recalled the mistakes they had made toward their peers and the director of their school and their sins before Jesus. They truly repented of all the mistakes they had ever made.

When they got back to the dormitory, the director asked them, "Where have you all been?" They replied that they hadn't been anywhere except where Nenilava was so that they might hear the words of Jesus. Then, they said, "We admit our rebellion and our errors and we ask for your forgiveness." The director was not so bold as to speak harsh words against them once he heard what they had to say! They continued to gather other friends to go to these meetings. At that time, there was a total change in many of the students. They put aside their mistaken and rebellious ways and the director was overjoyed.

When the director saw the change in these students, he invited Nenilava and her coworkers to the dormitory so he could see for himself how it was and what happened to make his pupils able to change their mistaken and rebellious ways so completely.

After this, the traveling evangelists were directed toward Brickaville, and there also many people came to them.

There was a blind man who was brought there by his family and then left all alone while they went back home. Nenilava approached this man and said to him, "Why have you come here?" The blind man responded, "I am blind, and I wish to be healed." Nenilava asked him, "Who is it that can open your eyes to see?" "Jesus can open my eyes to see," he said. "Didn't you come here to see a person?" Nenilava asked. "No," he said, "I came here to see Jesus." Nenilava then asked him, "Do you believe that Jesus has the power to open your eyes?" "Yes," the blind man said, "He has the power to do it if I believe." Nenilava said, "Repent before Jesus and he will heal your blindness."

For a whole hour the blind man wept. After crying such a long time, his eyes became clean and he said, "I can see!" Then he was taught how to use his hands and point to people with his finger. When the whole church saw this, they all wept for joy and thanked God for having permitted them to see the glory of Christ shown through the healing of this formerly blind man.

After the gathering was over, everyone returned to their homes, and the blind man whose eyes were opened also went back home. The people were all amazed and his whole family was filled to overflowing with joy.

After working for three days in Brickaville, the evangelist visitors left for Anivorano again, where they worked for a day and a half. Even though they only worked there for a very short time, many people repented, for they came to recognize their sins by hearing the word of God preached to them there. There was a lame man there, a non-Christian, who came to Jesus and was healed of his infirmity. Our days were truly grace-filled. The good news was on display and the world received a blessing.

The Spiritual Work in the Comoros Islands

When their spiritual work in Anivorano was completed, Nenilava and her companions went back up to Antananarivo again. When they got there, she found that they had received a telegram from the Comoros Islands. The pastor who received it showed it to Nenilava, and she decided that she had to go to the Comoros Islands. They worked there for only two weeks and then returned.

When they arrived there all the population was happy to welcome them: Comorean, French, and Malagasy residents. The first thing they did upon arrival was to register their presence with the gendarmerie and inform them of the old friends they had come to visit and the work they planned to do among the people.

The most amazing thing that Jesus did in the Comoros Islands concerned the Malagasy who had been exiled and were imprisoned there. The gendarmes encouraged the prisoners to attend worship so they could have clearer thoughts and get to know God. All of these prisoners were serving life sentences. When Nenilava and her coworkers came to visit the prisoners, they asked the prisoners what they most wished to ask of Jesus. They all responded that what they most wanted to ask Jesus was to be released from prison and to return to Madagascar.

As this was the unanimous desire of their hearts, Nenilava first asked Jesus, "Do you, O Jesus, agree with the lament of these twelve persons?" Jesus responded, "I do agree, and it is I who will open the hearts of the government authorities to release these prisoners in the coming month of August." The good news that Jesus had promised to set them free from prison was told to the prisoners. Nenilava then said to them, "Be of good courage, for this is the very word of Jesus!" When they heard this news, the prisoners asked, "Will all of us be freed, or only some of us?" Nenilava answered that they would all go free, according to the word of Jesus. Nenilava also told them that they should say nothing whatsoever of what would come to pass. "What you should do," she said, "is to pray to Jesus that he would carry out his plans for you, and you in return shall serve Him, for that is what would please him." With one voice they all said, "When we are free, we shall serve you, O Jesus, for all the rest of our lives!"

When the time came spoken of above, an official letter arrived from the government notifying the prison officials to release the twelve prisoners. When the gendarmerie saw this great thing that had happened, they sent a report to France. After their report was sent, a high-ranking French official arrived to see the work being done in the Comoros Islands. After he had seen the work, he flew by plane to Antananarivo. After the high-ranking government official had departed, the local government there gave full permission to Nenilava.[16] "This is the Lord's doing; it is

---

16. The Comoros Islands have a predominantly Muslim population. Hence, the local authorities may have been reluctant to permit Nenilava and her coworkers to engage in any public evangelism lest there be trouble, especially with a high-ranking official coming to visit.

marvelous in our eyes. Such knowledge is too wonderful for me; it is high; I cannot attain it" (Pss 118:23; 139:6).

It was not only in church that the team worked. They also visited in people's homes on an individual basis. One day, a blind *karana* invited them to his home. When they came to his house, they asked him the reason for the invitation. He explained that he needed some people of prayer to pray with him that his eyes might be opened to see. Before they entered into their spiritual work, they first preached to him the word of God that he would come to know God. When the sermon was over, he was reminded of all that he had done and the implications of his actions were made known to him. He had deceived his wife by telling her before their wedding that he was single, while in fact he was married to an Ambaniandro (Merina) resident in Antananarivo. It is she who had put a potion in his eyes and caused his present blindness. "If he confesses his errors," Jesus said, "and separates from his wife in Antananarivo, he will be healed." When the man agreed with these words and resolved to fulfill their demands, Nenilava prayed to Jesus for him and he was healed. Nenilava laid hands on him, prayed again, and then said to him that Jesus would do great things for him if he would only believe.

Then Nenilava went on to another house and met there another *karana* who complained to her, saying, "Please lift up my child in prayer to this God to whom you pray, because she is suffering a lot." Nenilava, however, asked him, "What is it that is making your child suffer, and what is her illness?" "She is not sick," her father responded. "She suffers so much in her mind because, one month after her wedding, her husband left her. That is why I ask you to pray for this child of mine, that her husband would come back to her." So Nenilava asked Jesus, "Is it still possible that the husband of this young woman would come back, so that I can know how to reply to him?" Jesus responded, "Yes, it is indeed possible that this young man will return. In fact, he is at this moment in Antananarivo, and he will surely return to live with her as his wife."

Then Nenilava told her that her husband would come back. The word of God was also preached to her so that she could know Jesus and to build up her faith. When this work was finished, they ended with prayer, and Nenilava departed from that house. One month after they had visited, the husband of the young woman came back and returned to her. She told Nenilava that her husband had indeed come back to her, just as God had foretold it to her!

After that, a good many Comoreans also came to see Nenilava at the house where she was staying. When they came, they talked about God and the word of God was preached. The fruit of these discussions was that a Comorean woman offered them a book which contained much information about the ancestral habits, customs, and writings about the Comorean religion.[17] This woman handed over the book without any reservations or conditions, and she offered her services in leading the Christian community in the region where she lived. She truly kept her promise and later became a catechist. She vowed that she would never separate herself from Jesus all the days of her life. The amazing thing about this is that her Comorean family did not agree to the founding of the Christian community in their neighborhood. When her family obstructed her in this way, she asked God to please take her from that place, as she suffered much from the arrogant and menacing words of her family. One year later, God granted her request and allowed her to leave that place.

The Spiritual Work in Marovoay

From the Comoros Islands, Nenilava went to work in Marovoay. When they got there, many sick people approached them. Many of them were mentally ill, and others had deep family problems. Their method of work in Marovoay did not change at all from what they practiced everywhere else they had previously worked: the word of God was proclaimed to all who came to them. Among those who came were a man and a woman, both of whom were lame but were healed. The woman who was healed later came to the revival center in Ankaramalaza, but the man returned home to Vangaindrano after he was completely healed.

The proclamation of the word of God and repentance were at the very root of healing the sick. There were many who were sick and who were engaged in spiritual warfare at the meetings, but it was only these two healings just mentioned that were total and complete. This makes us think of the words of the apostle Peter: "Truly I understand that God shows no partiality, but in every nation anyone who fears him and does what is right is acceptable to him" (Acts 10:34–35).

---

17. It is not clear from the text whether this refers to Islam or pre-Islamic ancestral beliefs of the Comoros Islands, similar to the *Sorabe* ("great writings") in Madagascar.

The Spiritual Work in Mahajanga

From Marovoay Nenilava went on to work in Mahajanga. A huge crowd came to welcome them upon their arrival. The church was too small because of the size of the crowd, and so the majority of people were outside in the church yard. The day began with a worship service and the preaching of the word of God to the many people who had gathered there. After the worship, the people all went back to their homes.

Because of the word of God that had been proclaimed, many were desirous of and thirsting for good things from Jesus. Among those most thirsty for this were the Christians who had been removed from the church rolls and no longer admitted to communion, along with non-Christians who were still not baptized.

On the third day that they worked there, many *karana* came to the prayer meetings, bringing their sick with them. Among those who came was a father of a child that had been sick from the time that she was in her mother's womb. God manifested his glory and power over this illness by healing the child. There was also a mute who was healed right before the eyes of a young woman[18] who had come simply to scrutinize what was going on in the movement.

Besides these, there was also a Greek man suffering from heart disease who came to them. He had already been operated on three times, twice in Antananarivo and once abroad. Despite all the operations he'd had, he was still far from really being healed. He wasn't able to get much sleep at night because of the throbbing of his heart. Sometimes his illness showed itself in fainting spells. For five years he had suffered like this. So he approached Nenilava, who put this question to him, "Do you know Jesus? "Of course I do," he said, "that's the reason that I have come to him, for he alone is the true Healer and he alone can save us from death and hell." Nenilava then said to him, "I will tell you what Jesus has to say to you, because you know *about* Jesus, but you don't believe." When the words of Jesus were shared with him, he understood them and believed them. Because of that, he repented and remembered all his errors. His sin was his disbelief and his transgressions against the laws of God.

Then Nenilava cast out in the name of Jesus the devils that were in him. The man shook constantly all during the time that the demons were

---

18. The text reads *mademoiselle,* suggesting that the woman in question was French or some other kind of European or possibly an American.

being cast out of him. As soon as the devils were driven out of him, he felt himself to be at peace and filled with joy, and he never again suffered from his throbbing chest pain. He returned three times to the house where Nenilava was staying. The word of God was preached to build up the faith that was in him and to help him recognize his sins. He received from Jesus the forgiveness of his sins. On the third day that they had worked with him he prayed to Jesus, saying, "I give glory to you, O God, for you who have healed me of my illness and gave me what I sought from you." That very day he entered into a Christian life and did not return to the sinful ways of his past. "From now on, my life shall be in God," he said. Ever since he continued in the life of faith.

After that a Frenchman also came. The calamity that happened to him was this: his eye had fallen out from its socket and was dangling down to his nose! As soon Nenilava saw this, she prayed to Jesus before doing anything else, in order to know the reason for this terrible thing having happened to him. Jesus said, "The reason for the removal of his eye from its socket is because of the wickedness of his eyes and the lasciviousness of his heart, for over the course of five years he has made his wife suffer, and she has seen nothing of all his money because he spent it all on other people. Because of this wickedness," Jesus said, "his wife has complained to me, saying: 'O Jesus, you know of my suffering, so I ask you to open his eyes to know of my suffering and misery.'" These words of Jesus were told to him, and he agreed that he had done these things: he had not given his wife any money, nor had he any dealings with her at all, and he hadn't given any thought to his responsibilities to the household.

So Nenilava said to him, "Do you agree to ask forgiveness of your wife and of God for the sins that you have committed?" "Yes," he responded, "I will ask forgiveness of Jesus and of my wife also, because my wife is a person who prays to God." Then they did their spiritual work in the name of Jesus, the demon that was in him was cast out, and that alone is why he came to have a clear mind. He shook so violently during the spiritual struggle that all the people in the house ran out because they were afraid of him. After that he came back to himself and said, "There was, indeed, an evil spirit in me. It caused me to suffer and to cause the suffering of my wife. However, I know that God hears prayer and forgives sinners. I will return to Marovoay," he said, "to ask her forgiveness, and then I will return here." He went there and asked forgiveness from his wife and his children. His wife accepted his repentance. She then prayed, "I truly thank you, O God, for my husband has come back and believes in you, our Savior and our Redeemer!"

For ten days they did their spiritual work on this man before they were able to get his left eye back into its place as God had first formed it. Jesus purified and healed his eye. The day after Jesus had healed his eye, he and his wife forgave one another once again in front of Nenilava. The woman wept continually because God had remembered her during her time of suffering. From now on, she also said, they would all become Protestants.[19] This great thing that Jesus had accomplished for this couple caused them to rejoice greatly. There are many ways by which Jesus calls people to come to him. He did this great thing so that this couple would believe in Jesus and be saved.

There was also a *karana* who was mute. This person was able to speak again because of Jesus' name, which is able to heal all illnesses. The healing of this person led the whole family to believe in the Lord Jesus. There was also another *karana* who had gone mad but recovered because of Jesus, who loves sinners.

Dear coworkers of Jesus! Proclaim Jesus and preach the truth so that all sinners may hear, for this Jesus is one in whom you can place your trust and who heals all who believe in him. Many people approached them because of the many illnesses of the flesh, and all who believed were healed.

At that time, the people asked that the area called Ndremisara might be destroyed, for it was a center of idolatry frequented by all people whether they were practitioners of Malagasy indigenous religion or Christians. Nenilava said to the people, "Jesus alone will destroy and burn it."

Later, this place where everyone, even those with advanced learning, prostrated themselves was ravaged by fire and totally destroyed. Many charms and fetishes were brought there by people. Some of these charms even spoke from within the big woven basket where they were located, while others kicked Nenilava's feet for, they said, "She is tormenting us!" The charms and amulets burned, and many people came to see them go up

---

19. The implication is that the family had previously been Catholic. Nenilava's ministry attracted Christians from all different denominations as well as other religions. During the height of her ministry, the Reformed were the most numerous Protestants, though the balance has shifted somewhat toward Lutherans, principally on account of the *fifohazana*. Ecumenical relations in Madagascar are fairly strong now; all the Christian churches participate in the Council of Christian Churches of Madagascar. It was formed in 1980, though at the time not so much for reasons of Christian unity as to have a unified voice against the government of Didier Ratsiraka.

in flames. A gendarme was present during the rite of *fandoroana ody*, the ritual act of burning charms and fetishes. Some of the charms cried out, "We are burning! We are burning!" There was, though, one charm that was not consumed by the fire despite the liter of gasoline that was poured on it. This charm was just too strong and confident in its stature and believed it could not be burned. Since this charm would not burn, Nenilava prayed and then they all sang the hymn called *Zanahary tsy mba tia ny fahaverezanao*, "The Creator God Does Not Desire for You To Be Lost."[20] When the time of prayer was over, the charm was burned once again. This time it was totally burned to nothing. When the charm burned up, everyone was amazed to see that Jesus was very powerful indeed!

The owner of the charm said that the charm had already killed five people with his help. He rejoiced also that his charm was burned, because he was afraid lest it turn against him and kill both him and his family. Because of this, he offered himself to become a Christian and serve Jesus. He asked forgiveness from the church for what he had done in murdering people and his deception of the nation by this totally empty thing.

The great works done by God in Mahajanga led many people to accept Jesus and to receive the Holy Spirit.

The Spiritual Work at Ambatomanga

When they finished their spiritual work in Mahajanga, Nenilava returned to Antananarivo again. From there they went down to Ambatomanga where they worked for a month. Preaching the word of God, strengthening people by the laying-on of hands, and casting out demons were done there also. Many people came each time they met to hear the word of God. Many sick also came, seeking healing. One of these was a man who was lame. He trusted in Jesus and believed in his power and so was healed and made well.

Also coming there was a woman claiming to be Christian who actually served an idol. When Nenilava preached and cast out demons from many, this woman also approached her. When Nenilava laid hands upon her, the devil in her pitched her about violently and she lost her mind. After some days, her family brought her to the house where Nenilava was staying. Jesus then said to Nenilava that amulets were buried in her house and that they must be removed. The woman agreed immediately that this was so. She also decided to take all the charms and amulets out of her

20. *Tiona sy Fihirana*, #255.

home and offer them up to Nenilava. She was then completely healed because she had left her sinful ways.

If Christians continue to be of two minds, they will certainly not be saved, for God does not tolerate evil, especially in those who bear his name! God says in 2 Chronicles 7:14, "If my people who are called by my name humble themselves, and pray and seek my face and turn from their wicked ways, then I will hear from heaven and will forgive their sin and heal their land."

The Spiritual Work in Ambatolampy

Nenilava went down again to Ambatolampy and worked there. Great crowds of people came to attend the church meetings and many who were weak in faith repented and returned to church again when they heard the word of God proclaimed. Many government workers came and entered into the church. For the missionary elders it was a real joy to see each of the boarders from the dormitories repent of their rebellious ways. The pastor of the local parish worked together with Nenilava for two weeks. He encouraged the Christians to receive the grace of God that had been brought to them.

Young people were being called from the regions of Antananarivo, Marovoay, Maroantsetra, Antanifotsy, Antsirabe, and Morondava. Faith in Jesus is the true life, and only those who believe in him are truly blessed. So go forward together with him, for only those who go with Jesus will conquer and have peace in their hearts. Trust the one who calls you by name, because he is the guarantor of all your days, and you too should be a witness to his name!

Spiritual Work in Ivohibe

It was at Vondrozo that the missionary came to get Nenilava in order to bring her to work in Ivohibe. She began her spiritual work in the church the same day as her arrival there. Mamavao alternated with Nenilava in preaching the word of God in Ivohibe.

Huge crowds came to attend the prayer services, but the majority of the people who came, above all the government officials, came only to see something new. When they heard the word of God, however, they were all convicted of their sin and truly repented. There was a person with edema who came to Jesus and was healed. There was another person with mental disorders healed by the power of Jesus, who wants all people to be saved. Separated couples were reconciled.

There was even a pastor who said to Jesus, "Did I not ask you, O Jesus, for a wife who would work together with me and give me offspring?" Because they didn't have any children, their household was shattered. The pastor was really ready to fight with Jesus and said, "I asked you for a wife. Why did you give me this woman with a dead womb?"

After he had put this question to Jesus, Nenilava and Mamavao began to pray for him. When they had finished praying, Nenilava told him the word of God for him, and she discussed with him the manner in which God directs our lives. Nenilava said, "God blessed the man and the woman and promised to give them many children. Because of this God will give you a child by your wife." Jesus then spoke directly to Nenilava, saying that he would give a child to the pastor. Then, after hearing what Jesus had to say to her about the pastor, Nenilava said to him, "Your wife will have a child. Believe that God will accomplish all your desires, for he has heard you." Despite this assurance from Jesus, the pastor still didn't believe it and said, "I won't believe any of this unless I see it with my own eyes, for I have lost confidence in Jesus." Nenilava spoke to him again, saying, "Believe it. For everything is possible with Jesus, and what is impossible for people is possible for God." When the pastor heard that he just said, "I will believe it, and I will wait in hopefulness for the fulfillment of all that was said to me today."

One month later, his wife was with child. When she told her husband about it, however, the pastor argued with his wife and said to her, "Maybe you are just lying to me, woman!" However, by the time his wife was three months into the pregnancy, he hurried to send a letter of thanks and of repentance to Jesus, care of Nenilava, for his unbelief and for not accepting the words that were spoken to him. Nenilava answered his letter and encouraged him to trust, believe, and rejoice. From that time on, the pastor vowed to serve Jesus for the rest of his days. By the time of the writing of this book, he and his wife had five children. This true life story shows us that the Lord hears whatever we ask of him as he has promised (John 16:24).

The Spiritual Work in Toliara

The fame of this servant of God was heard about throughout the whole island. Because of this, every region thirsted for a visit from Nenilava. The town of Toliara desired to have a visit and they got one. When Nenilava and her coworkers arrived there, they went and stayed at the home of the pastor. Before they began their work in town, they first visited the missionary elders to tell them of their arrival. At two in the afternoon that day, they began their spiritual work. The majority of people who came to them and with whom they worked were those who were not Christians and the prostitutes of the city. Thus the word of Jesus in Matthew 21:31b was fulfilled, "Truly, I say to you, the tax collectors and the prostitutes go into the kingdom of God before you."

Many among these people repented when they heard the word of God. After the preaching, the work of strengthening and the casting out of demons followed, and many demons were cast out of people, causing them to writhe on the ground in the church. Everyone was astonished to see the demons cast out of people. Then they laid hands on everyone, after which they dispersed.

Even though the meeting had ended, the spiritual work continued at the house where Nenilava was staying. At that time some *karana*, Arabs, and a few Malagasy brought their sick there. What really amazed people was to see these *karana* and Arabs who had the evil spirit called *tromba*, which was very powerful and caused their victims to shake terribly. This *tromba* spirit ruled over Toliara. The majority of the population was possessed by it because the people treated it like a god, praying to it and serving it always.

Throughout their whole stay at that place, all those who were possessed by the *tromba* came to the meetings that they might be healed. One of those who came was a Catholic woman who was very weak on account of the *tromba* that was in her. She couldn't stand up and so she was unable to come to church. She just had to wait at the home of the pastor where Nenilava was staying. She stayed in that place until she was healed. When she was healed of her disease, she became a Protestant. There were also those who suffered from lung diseases such as tuberculosis that were healed by Jesus and became well.

The other amazing things done by Jesus were that many active demons were cast out, and many works were done in the church. Many people who were possessed repented and became Christians because of the word of God that was proclaimed to them. There were also those who realized they needed to return to church and so they became confirmands.

For one month they did their spiritual work in Toliara, and there were many who repented. There were even seven people who traveled to Ankaramalaza and became servants of God and are even now shepherds in the revival movement. Four became *mpiandry* or shepherd-evangelists, while three of them haven't.

There was a *karana* boy of twelve years who had been weak since birth and was brought by his parents to church. Nenilava asked his parents, "What is the reason for your coming here?" "We have brought our weak child," they said. "To whom exactly have you brought him?" asked Nenilava. "We have brought him to Jesus," they responded, "the one who has healed many, so that our child may be freed of this weakness in his body." "Do you all believe that Jesus can heal this weakness in your child?" "We believe," they said, "that our child will be able to stand by the power of Jesus." So Nenilava prayed. After the prayer Nenilava said to the child, "Arise, in the name of Jesus of Nazareth!" He arose and walked all around the church. His parents were overjoyed and became and remained Christians.

The Spiritual Work in North Ranotsara

Spiritually speaking, this was a place of total darkness. There were some church people there but their religion was just a habit. They knew nothing at all about the meaning of repentance. It was not until the second day of their work in that town that the power of God began to work. Bit by bit their minds became clear and they realized their sinfulness.

After three days, among those who came to Nenilava were some children of a local midwife in town who were twins. In the church each one there was reminded of their sins and repented. These two boys, however, who were about twelve years old, both saw angels, one on Nenilava's right and the other on her left. Everyone in the church saw the light, but only these two boys saw the angels. When the boys saw them they began to call out, saying, "There are angels, there are angels!" There was also a woman there who opposed strongly what the boys said, insisting that what they said was not true. "If that's really true," she said, "we would be able to see them, too!" The children didn't agree but just called out all the more, "We see them. We see them. And we must tell you so!"

On the way home, this woman kept scolding the boys. At that time, however, there was another person who said to the woman, "We shouldn't scold the children so, lest God wanted to show them and only them this thing." When the young woman heard these words, she fell silent and stopped scolding the children.

When this woman went to sleep that night, the room where she slept got bright and she grew frightened. After sitting up she saw the two angels, one above her head, while the other who was near her feet clutched her hand. The angels didn't depart from their places, so she went to see her mother trembling with fear and told her what had happened. When her mother heard what she said, her mother directed her to go quickly to her room, saying, "Go back, for this is a blessing coming to pay you a visit." So she hastened back to her room and knelt down between the two angels who had appeared to her. When the young woman had prayed and said the amen, the angels immediately disappeared and the room became dark again. After the angels left, the woman was unable to sleep. Instead she began to repent. This woman was among those who truly changed, even though she had been one of those most against the revival.

The next evening there was a family prayer service and one of the angels appeared. No one else in the house saw the angels but her. Then the angel said to the woman, "Do not be like those who do not believe, but believe so that you will not be lost."

The Spiritual Work in Vohipeno

As we said in the beginning of this story, Nenilava is a native of the district of Vohipeno. In view of the great works that took place there, this district should be praised to the highest heaven. That isn't what we see if we look at the harvest overall. Among the leaders who worked with her, you would expect to see the firstfruits of the work, but that was not so. So near to the source of light, many remained in darkness. Thanks be to God that the majority of the population received her well and expanded the revival all through the district, and each day the Lord added to the number of those being saved.

When Nenilava began to visit other places outside the district, however, she could no longer visit as often in the district of Vohipeno. More and more, the only time she was able to visit was during the annual gathering of the revival movement. This was a disaster for the district. The lag time between visits slowly but surely brought about a coldness of heart in many and resulted in the diminishment of the district.

The Center of Revival at Ankaramalaza

Ankaramalaza is a place located about 20 kilometers north of Vohipeno. Once it was a place where zebu were raised and people farmed. Long before, Mosesy Tsirefo had asked Malady, the father of Nenilava, if he could cultivate coffee, bananas, oranges, and rice there. Then after that, Mosesy built a house for himself, his family, and some people in his employ. In 1935 Mosesy Tsirefo's first wife died. In 1936 he married Germaine Volahavana.

On October 14, 1949, Mosesy Tsirefo died. Before he died, though, he planned to sell his property. At the time Jesus asked Nenilava why this land was going to be sold. Nenilava responded that she didn't know. Then Jesus said to Nenilava, "Tell Mosesy that he is a Judas if he sells this property, for it is not his. That place is mine. That place is my property, and if he sells it, it would be like selling me! People will come to this place and it will not look then as it does today." Mosesy Tsirefo then canceled his plan to sell the land and didn't do so.

It was only in the year 1953 that this place started being called a *toby*, because a great many sick people had been coming there. So the Toby Ankaramalaza was created, and its population continued to grow from day to day. Now there is even a church and a pastor there who is in charge of the spiritual work. Each year a massive number of people come to visit and attend the great annual revival gathering of the Toby Ankaramalaza. Many come also from different nations and tribes to stay there during the gathering.

When Nenilava began to work, twenty-two young people, both men and women, were with her in Ankaramalaza. Some of them became pastors. From that time on, little by little, people came to the *toby*. Most of them were sick and looking for healing. Some of the young people were stubborn and rebellious, swimming in their mad schemes while devouring the possessions of their parents. Instead of staying at home, they persisted in robbing other people's things. Their parents didn't know what they could do about it, so they brought them to Nenilava. These young people were taken care of and worked with at the *toby*, where they were all healed and freed from their rebellious natures. They did not want to go back home afterwards, because their former illnesses and unease with life had shown them their true calling.

Other people received the call of God when they brought their sick family members to the *toby*. After the healing of their family members, they decided to stay at the *toby*, even though their family members went back home. Up to this day, the number of people residing at Ankaramalaza has grown tremendously. Some of these were young people who received a call from Jesus and decided to stay, while others were the sick who had been healed and grown to feel at home and at peace there. At the time of writing there were thirty-two *mpiandry* at the Toby Ankaramalaza, of whom twelve were young people and twenty adults. There were also ten others, candidates preparing for their consecration as *mpiandry*. There were still others preparing for consecration at the Forty-Man School[21] in Vangaindrano and at the Lutheran Graduate School of Theology at Ivory, Fianarantsoa. At this same period, more than four hundred people lived at the *toby*. They were all entirely supported by the *toby*: fed, clothed, taxes paid, and taught the word of God.

Pastor Ramerlina and his wife were responsible for the teaching of the word of God, which took place twice a week at the *toby*. The *toby* was under the oversight of a district of the church and its pastor. Pastor Ndrona Hederson was the district pastor before he died. Afterwards Pastor Soliman Ben-Abdala was the one in charge of the Vohipeno District. The sons and daughters of Ankaramalaza are now scattered throughout out the island, proclaiming the gospel of salvation.

Each year many guests come to visit Ankaramalaza. When guests come to visit the *toby*, this is how they are welcomed. The *mpiandry* of the *toby* go out together to welcome the guests at the village gateway. The welcome is accompanied by songs, and a procession leads the guests to a large mango tree at the center of the village. There the feet of all the people who come to the *toby* are washed—no exceptions. After this reception, which is a mark of honor, the guests are led to the rooms in the guest house to which they have been assigned. Once they have settled in, there is a time of prayer and the word of God is preached to the guests. There is a person responsible for taking care of the guests at all times. Each day there is a time of prayer that takes place at the *toby* beginning at seven thirty in the evening and lasting until eleven, sometimes even longer.

---

21. Forty-Man Schools were training centers for catechists and evangelists in the Malagasy Lutheran Church, following the pattern first set by Lutheran missionaries, who followed the pattern for education set earlier by the Friends Foreign Mission Society and the London Missionary Society. "Forty-Man School" meant a secondary school, graduation from which was required to study at a Bible school and later a seminary. The term was chosen for its biblical connotations: forty years in the wilderness as a time of preparation. See *Jobily Faha-Dimam-polo*, 9. See also *From Darkness to Light*, 109. There is, however, a typo in this source, which reads "*49-lahy*" instead of "*40-lahy*."

It is a great responsibility to care for all these people in the *toby*. The creation of the *toby* was not the idea of any human person, as already stated, but was totally the plan of Jesus. One can say that, in reality, it was really Jesus who built, supports, and guarantees it. Thus, Jesus has directed the thoughts of many persons about how they can take a part in maintaining the *toby*. Male and female elders of the government as well as Christians overseas have been pressed by the Spirit to take their part in support of the *toby*. We should also note that, in addition to the great number of notable people who have been cared for and healed at the *toby*, there have also been many children. At the time of writing about 110 were schooled there. The teachers of these children were Claire Razanarivo and her friend Lina.

It is good to be reminded in a special way of the amazing story concerning the death of Mosesy Tsirefo. When he died and left this world, he came to a gateway. When he tried to get through the gateway, however, he could not pass through because his shoulders prevented him and the passage was too narrow. He strove to pass through, trying many ways to do so. He often turned himself sideways to be able to enter but he couldn't, for the gateway would turn in different directions so that it was facing the wrong way and he was unable to pull off his attempt to get through. In the end, an angel invited him to return to earth so that he could be reconciled to his wife, for there was something that saddened her about which they needed to forgive each other. The body of Mosesy Tsirefo was still lying in the hospital when he returned from heaven.

So he lifted the sheet that had been placed over his head. When the people present saw this, they were all seized by fear and asked him, "Why have you come back like this again?" He responded, as stated above, that he had not been able to enter the gate of heaven because he had not yet received forgiveness from his wife for all that he had done to cause her suffering. So he said to his wife, "I ask your forgiveness for all the suffering I have caused you. If I am lost, it will be because of those things." In response, Nenilava said to him that she forgave him all that Jesus still held against him that was keeping him from entering into heaven. After these words of complete forgiveness were spoken to him, he immediately died and departed for good, never to return.

Oh, dear readers, presenting us with this true story, the Lord reminds us that in his eyes forgiveness has great importance. If it is not completed here on earth, it will prevent us from entering into heaven. So then, let us all forgive the sins of our friends, because, if not, our heavenly Father will not forgive us, either (Matt 18:32–35).

The Spiritual Work in Fort Dauphin

Ever since 1957 many Christians in Fort Dauphin had planned to send for Nenilava to come to the southern part of the island. In 1958 two pastors had a chance meeting with Nenilava, so they took the opportunity to reiterate to her this long-expressed thirst. But at that moment she was not free to speak about when she might come to meet with them, and she was sad that she could not say all that was in her heart. They could only say a few words to her, asking her to please come also to Fort Dauphin. When she heard their wishes and request, she agreed that she would one day go there.

It was five years after this conversation, in 1963, that the visit of this servant of God to Fort Dauphin finally came about. Ever since that year, Nenilava and her coworkers have continued to work in the south. They have visited and done their spiritual work in many places, including Fort Dauphin, Manafiafy, Manambaro, Amboasary, Tsivory, Tsihombe, Beloha, Bekily, Manentenina, Ranomafana, Isoanala, and Betroka.

The proclamation of the gospel is at the root of all the work wherever Nenilava goes. The Lord Jesus works together with her, and that is why her work continually bears much fruit. Her way of working in the south was no different than in all the other places she had worked in terms of the fruits seen and displayed. Many Christians who had left the church or grown cold in the faith once again returned to church. Many non-Christians repented and gave up their charms and amulets and became Christians. Many possessed by demons and many sick people were set free and healed and came to believe in Jesus the savior. All the pastors at every one of these locations are witnesses to these things.

By the grace of God the spiritual works of the revival continue to progress without ceasing. The number of *mpiandry* continues to grow. There are those who train at Ankaramalaza or at other places. Many others train at their local churches. At the time of writing, Betroka had a *toby*, too, and in 1970 the *toby* in Manambaro consecrated eleven *mpiandry*. As it says in Psalm 118:23: "This is the Lord's doing; it is marvelous in our eyes." It is now the day of the Holy Spirit, and that is why many sinners have been visited, because God "desires all people to be saved and to come to the knowledge of the truth" (1 Tim 2:4).

Words in Closing

Oh, dear readers, all this has been an examination of the story and works of Nenilava in the many different places where she has gone, and her ministry continued even after. As you have read this simple story, I hope that each and every one of you has not seen in it anything other than Jesus and him alone. The time is close at hand, and Jesus the Lord is close to appearing. "I am coming soon," he says. "Hold fast what you have, so that no one may seize your crown" (Rev 3:11).

The writer: Pastor Zakaria Tsivoery
Fort Dauphin, 20 August 1970

Text translated from Malagasy into French
by Pastor Mamy Andriamahenina
Paris, 20 May 2004

Chapter 2: The Rest of the Story (1971–1998)

—James B. Vigen

THE STORY YOU HAVE just read was set down by Zakaria Tsivoery, a pastor of the Southeast Synod of the Malagasy Lutheran Church (MLC). At the time he wrote Nenilava's story he was serving at Fihaonana Church, the oldest Lutheran congregation in southern Madagascar, founded in 1888 by the first American Lutheran missionary pastor to Madagascar, John Peter Hogstad.[1] Tsivoery was also instrumental in the establishment of the Toby Nenilava in Fort Dauphin.

According to the Tsivoery manuscript, Nenilava made many trips to Antananarivo, lodging in the Soanierana neighborhood. However, in 1971 her followers acquired a property for her base of operations in another capital neighborhood called 67 Hectares. The curious name comes from the fact that the government purchased a tract of sixty-seven hectares in the 1960s, as more housing was needed in the capital, especially for university students. Nenilava's address was Logement #237.[2] From that time on she no longer lived permanently in the isolated rural town of Ankaramalaza, possibly on account of concern from her disciples about her health.

---

1. There was an older congregation formed before Hogstad's arrival connected to the Merina Garrison in Fort Dauphin. It was founded by the Merina governor and was served by a London Missionary Society-trained catechist only. When Hogstad arrived, the governor turned the pastoral leadership over to him. Hogstad quickly realized, however, that being so closely aligned with the Merina governor was detrimental to his mission to evangelize the indigenous Tanosy people he had come to serve. He then established his own Lutheran church outside the garrison walls, where Fihaonana Church still stands today, though the original building was destroyed in a cyclone. Tsivoery served at Fihaonana from 1951 to 1980, after which he lived at the Toby Nenilava until his death there on December 1, 1994.

2. *Tobilehibe Ankaramalaza*, 18–19. All quotes from this and other books written in Malagasy are my translation.

In time a small house church developed around Nenilava for a practical reason: when she and her companions tried to walk from 67 Hectares to the only Lutheran church in the city, located in Ambatovinaky, her route was impeded by all the people who approached her. Eventually, Dr. Rakoto Andrianarijaona, the senior pastor at Ambatovinaky, took charge of the house church at 67 Hectares, which was at the time considered a part of the Ambatovinaky parish.[3] When the congregation came to outgrow that space as well, it formed the second Lutheran congregation in Antananarivo, going by the same name as its neighborhood.[4] Between 1976 and 1978, Dr. Péri Rasolondraibe assisted Dr. Andrianarijaona in the ministry of the church.[5] Before long worship attendance was even greater there than at Ambatovinaky. Malagasy Lutherans do not care for lay assistants nor for stations around the church for distributing the sacrament of the altar, so the one monthly communion service can require upwards of six pastors and an hour and a half to accommodate all communicants at the rail!

In the years to come, Nenilava only rarely joined in Sunday morning worship. She felt that her presence caused too much of a distraction. The audio of the service would instead be piped into her rooms at #237. After worship she would receive visitors asking for prayer, advice, healing, or blessings. While residing at 67 Hectares Nenilava continued, on occasion, to make short trips around the country. She always returned to Ankaramalaza for the annual meeting in August for the consecration of new shepherds.

In February 1973 Nenilava made a trip with several companions to a northern suburb of the capital called Ambohibao. They had already been looking for some time for a location to establish a new *toby* with enough space for people to lodge while awaiting assistance. 67 Hectares had already become too confined a location for a healing ministry, since most of the available land had been taken up by the large church building

---

3. *Tobilehibe Ankaramalaza*, 18.

4. The reason that there was only one Lutheran church in Madagascar's largest city at that time dates back to the so-called Comity Agreements made by Protestant churches and missionary societies delineating their respective mission fields. The signatories agreed to stay out of each others' fields. However, there was a provision for a single congregation to be located in the capital city of the nation for representational purposes.

5. In 1981, the house church of 67 Hectares moved to a new building in the same area of 67 Hectares. It was named Hope Lutheran Church/67 Hectares. Then years later, it became a parish of its own, with five other, smaller congregations affiliated with it. In 2010, when Dr. Péri Rasolondraibe was the senior pastor of Hope Lutheran Church/67 Hectares, it had become the largest Lutheran congregation in the whole of Africa with a membership of 10,300 parishioners.

eventually built there. According to Nenilava, Jesus led them to a side street just off the main road to the airport in Ambohibao. A retired pastor named Rakotonizao had some land for sale, so Nenilava and her associates went to the house and asked to meet with him. He said that he did, indeed, have land for sale. After prayer and some conversation, Nenilava asked the pastor how much he was asking for the land. He replied, "Well for *you*, I'll sell it for . . ." and then named the sum that he and his family had previously agreed upon. Nenilava, however, knew exactly how much money they had available, because she had inquired of the treasurer of the movement before setting out. She replied to the pastor, "Jesus doesn't agree to your price; this is how much he is offering you." And, amazingly, without bartering one bit, the pastor agreed to the exact price![6] After the sale of the land was completed, the movement began slowly remodeling the existing house as a residence for Nenilava and a future *toby*. It took fourteen years before that became a reality.

In 1973 Nenilava traveled abroad. Tsivoery reports her short trip to the Comoros Islands, but this time Nenilava visited the United States, Norway, and France. There were two main reasons for the extended trip. The first was that Oliver and Gene Carlson, former missionaries in southern Madagascar and ardent supporters of the revival work, had invited her to come. Oliver was also one of those responsible for inviting Nenilava to visit Fort Dauphin for the first time. Serving as director of Zion Harbor Lutheran Bible Camp on Leech Lake in northern Minnesota, he probably hoped to raise funds for the movement through her visit. However, because of the views of some American missionaries in Madagascar that circulated around, he was sternly warned by church leadership *not* to arrange for Nenilava to speak in any Lutheran congregation. The only one she ended up visiting was one that hosted the wedding of a former Madagascar missionary kid named Mark Walters.

As a result, Nenilava spent most of her time in the U.S. at the camp. No one who met her failed to be impressed by her, the younger American campers included. Yet as far as the younger campers were concerned, the most memorable event was when she and Razanamiadana, a *mpiandry*-evangelist who accompanied her on the trip, took their laundry down to

---

6. *Tobilehibe Ankaramalaza*, 33. The amount the pastor and his family wanted was "*sivy Alina sy Roa Hetsy*" (290,000, presumably in Malagasy francs) but Nenilava offered only "*sivy alina*" (90,000). In 1973 currency, the asking price was $6,505, and Nenilava got it for $2,019.

the lake and washed their clothes in it; then, Malagasy-style, beat them dry over a rock![7]

The second reason for Nenilava's foreign trip was a formal invitation to visit Norway, where she was awarded one of the nation's highest honors, the St. Olaf Medal, by King Olav V himself.[8] When the king asked her to describe her work, she told him, "I preach the gospel, I heal the mentally ill, I educate young delinquents, I raise up infants and the elderly."[9] She also visited at the headquarters of the Norwegian Missionary Society in Stavanger and spoke at several churches there.

En route back to Madagascar, Nenilava and Razanamiadana spent some time in France but nothing has been recorded about their time there. In those days there were not many international flights to Madagascar, so they may have only been waiting for their plane or visiting with the many Malagasy migrants residing in France.

Nenilava's next important trip was a return to Fort Dauphin toward the end of 1978 and early 1979. Jesus had revealed to her that there was a property located just on the edge of town where he wanted her to establish another *toby*.

As the revival movement had grown in numbers over the years, it became apparent that the small *toby* in Manambaro, twenty-five kilometers west of Fort Dauphin and consisting of only two small houses with no land to expand, could not serve the area properly. So during Nenilava's visit the revival committee sought to locate a larger plot of land upon which to build a proper *toby*, capable of receiving people in need of healing of various kinds.

When Nenilava arrived, the committee met with her to decide where the new *toby* should be located. "No need to discuss that," said Nenilava, for Jesus had already told her exactly where he wanted his new healing center to be located! It seemed that an elderly expatriate named André Doyen had a very large and beautiful estate for sale right on the outskirts

---

7. Personal communication with Christopher Carlson, son of Oliver and Gene Carlson, August 6, 2020. Oliver (d. July 15, 2020) was a second-generation missionary to Madagascar, having grown up there from 1922 to 1937 and then serving for two stints, from 1954 to 1967 and again from 1983 to 1988.

8. Austnaberg, *Shepherds and Demons*, 54n156. There is some uncertainty about this St. Olaf Medal. I wrote to the palace asking for a copy of the record of the award, only to be informed there is actually no record of Nenilava receiving it. It may be that the NMS requested this honor be given to her, but the palace did not agree to the request; or it may be a clerical error on the part of the palace administration. We simply do not know.

9. Rasoanahimanga, "Nenilava," para. 25.

of Fort Dauphin. Doyen wished to sell his estate since he was returning home to Europe.

On Monday, January 1, 1979, Nenilava and other *mpiandry* met with the land owner and discussed the purchase of his estate. Doyen was asking for twenty million Malagasy francs, a huge amount at that time. After showing them around, Doyen addressed Nenilava, calling her *"ma soeur,"* the typical French address for a Roman Catholic nun! He told her he would be most happy if she were the one to purchase his property. No deal was agreed upon at that time, however. The committee returned to their meeting place to ask whether it was really possible for them to raise the amount asked. When the word got out, people in town mocked the *mpiandry*, saying, "Where will you few Christians ever find twenty million Malagasy francs?" Many on the committee agreed with this sentiment. However, Nenilava put an end to all discussion and hesitation when she quoted from Deuteronomy 1:8, "See, I have set the land before you. Go in and take possession of the land"! The committee met with Doyen and signed a contract with him, and he turned over the deed to the property to the committee of the *toby*. Donations were received from all over Madagascar, Europe, and the U.S. to help pay for this *toby*.

The anniversary of the *toby* is held on January 15 because that was the day Nenilava first visited it. The committee also asked Nenilava what the *toby* should be named. She declined to answer, saying the *toby* membership should pray about it and choose a name for themselves. Many were suggested, but the *mpiandry* finally decided to name it after Nenilava herself.[10]

Perhaps the most controversial event in Nenilava's life after her early years came on August 2, 1983, when she was presented before the attendees of the annual meeting of the Fifohazana revival movement at Ankaramalaza for her consecration as a prophetess of God.[11] She was dressed in robes that the *mpiandry* had styled for her based on the description of those of the high priest Aaron in Exodus 28. The robe was woven of fine Malagasy silk, dyed gold, blue, and purple. Embroidered into the cloth were the names of the twelve tribes of Israel. Sewn into the robe were various precious stones, all found in Madagascar, including emeralds, sapphires, diamonds, amethysts, agates, and topazes. Upon her head,

---

10. *Tobilehibe Ankaramalaza*, 44–47.

11. This event, called in Malagasy a *fanokanana*, was interpreted by Malagasy theologians who officiated at the event as being something like the prophetic, symbolic actions performed by many Old Testament prophets (cf. Isa 20:2–3; Jer 27–28; Hos 1:2; 3:1).

instead of the turban of Exodus 28, she wore a crown of silver with a cross atop it, inscribed with the words, "Holy to the Lord." All of the materials necessary for the making of these things were found in Madagascar, along with the artisans who accepted the charge.[12]

At this time, the Fifohazana movement was so strong and popular in Madagascar that no missionary dared oppose it anymore, as some had in earlier years. Still, this investiture was thought to be theologically dubious by many Westerners. As a result, not a single representative of the various missions working with the MLC attended the ceremony.[13] Lotera Fabien, dean of the Lutheran Graduate School of Theology at Ivory, Fianarantsoa, acknowledges that "this prophetic symbol was a stumbling block to some theologians but was accepted by many others because they saw that her doing this did *not* mean she would be consecrated as a High Priest, but rather it was merely as a manifestation of her consecration [as a prophetess]." Her followers supported the rite because Nenilava told them that Jesus himself had ordered her to accept this public recognition.[14] According to Nenilava, Jesus had first revealed this to her in 1954 after the official recognition of the revival movement by the MLC. But she hesitated to go forward with it, for fear it might be misunderstood. Jesus reminded her of his desire in 1963 when she first visited Fort Dauphin, but again she hesitated. Finally, in 1974 she spoke openly of this revelation to her followers, and preparations were begun to see the matter through. Still, it was nearly a decade until it came to pass.[15]

Nenilava was directly responsible for the creation of one other *toby* during her lifetime, which is the only one officially recognized outside of Madagascar, the Toby Pouru St. Remy in the Ardennes region of France. That it is in France should come as no surprise: somewhere between 25,000 and 50,000 people of Malagasy origin are now resident citizens of

---

12. Quoted in Nielsen and Hestad, "Christian Revivalism and Political Imagination," 204.

13. Nielsen and Hestad, "Christian Revivalism and Political Imagination," 204. The three missions were the Norwegian, the Danish, and the American Lutheran Church.

14. Fabien, "Malagasy Lutheran Church," 3.

15. Jaona and Yvonne, "The Prophet Nenilava," 5. See also the privately published pamphlet from the Toby Ankaramalaza: Rakatoarivony, et al., *Tantaran'ny Zava-Niseho*, written by three Malagasy seminary professors—Rakotoarivony Stephenson, Rakoto Endor Modeste, and Rasolondraibe Péri—and the General Secretary of the MLC, Rabemanantsoa Noel. All four are pastors and consecrated *mpiandry*, and three hold PhDs.

France.[16] There are, in fact, so many Malagasy Lutherans in France that they have organized themselves into a legal association of churches and appealed to the MLC to accept them as an officially recognized synod. This was provisionally agreed to in 1993.[17] It was these congregations that invited Nenilava to come for a second visit to France in 1980, along with two *mpiandry*, Rabarihoela Malala and Raharivelo Georgette, and the children of one of these women.[18]

However, at this time there was not a Malagasy Lutheran congregation in the town of Pouru St. Remy. How, then, did there come to be a *toby* in that place? Raoelison Helimirina, known as Dr. Lala, tells the story. Her father, Randriambololona Simiona, was a medical doctor in Pouru St. Remy. At some point in 1978 he "rediscovered the gospel."[19] This led the family to read through the Acts of the Apostles. Someone mentioned an amazing woman known as Nenilava. Simiona had an opportunity to meet her when he traveled to Madagascar for a week in February 1979 to attend the funeral of his sister. He got an audience with her at her home at #237. During their time together, Jesus told Nenilava that he wanted the good doctor consecrated immediately so that he could return to France as a *mpiandry* and begin the work of the movement there.[20]

In November 1979 Dr. Lala herself had the opportunity to travel to Madagascar as part of her medical training through a grant from the Raoul

---

16. It is hard to determine the exact number, as a 1978 law "specifically banned the collection and computerized storage of race-based data without the express consent of the interviewees or a waiver by a state committee. France therefore collects *no* census or other data on the race (or ethnicity) of its citizens." Bleich, "Race Policy in France," para. 3.

17. The Executive Committee of the MLC meeting in Toliara, June 8–13, 1993, agreed to receive this body as part of the MLC but not yet as a fully equal synod. It was rather to be supervised by the Executive Committee of the MLC. In 2008 the MLC Churchwide Assembly meeting at Morondava on September 3–12, 2008, accepted these Malagasy Lutherans as a full-fledged synod with their own elected leadership. By this time, congregations outside of France were also added to the overseas synod. The European Synod of the MLC consists of four districts: Strasbourg, Marseille, Paris, and Île-de-France. Several parishes in Canada are also included in the synod. Private communication with Rakontondrazaka Habberstad, president of the Synodam-paritany Fiangonana Loterana Malagasy any Europa (SPFLME), July 28, 2020.

18. *Tobilehibe Ankaramalaza*, 55.

19. This history can be found on the *toby* website: https://spflme-tobypouru.org/notre-histoire/.

20. Toby Pouru Saint-Remy, "Notre Histoire." To my knowledge, Simiona is the only person ever to be consecrated a *mpiandry* without the mandatory two-year training period, other than Nenilava herself.

Follereau Foundation. She also met with Nenilava and received a blessing from her in January 1980. Not to be outdone, Randriambololona—Simiona's wife and Dr. Lala's mother—also traveled to Madagascar in May 1980 and spent time at the Toby Ankaramalaza. Before returning to France, Nenilava shared with Randriambololona that Jesus wanted Nenilava herself to go visit Pouru St. Remy with the family.[21]

On July 7, 1980, Nenilava and her small entourage arrived in Paris. They spent two days in the home of Dr. Lala in Bagneux, then proceeded on to Pouru St. Remy on July 9, 1980, staying at the doctor's home until November 7, 1980. Throughout that period people came to see her from all around France and Belgium. Nenilava and her companions preached, counseled, healed, and cast out demons, just as they had done in so many other places.[22]

Perhaps in response to the many people hungry for the word of God and healing, Nenilava told the people that the Lord wanted a *toby* to be established at Pouru St. Remy. It was decided that this should be done while Nenilava was still with them, formally dedicating the *toby* as well as consecrating several *mpiandry* in order to begin the work. On August 17, 1980, four *mpiandry* were thus consecrated: Randriambololona Rahely from Pouru St. Remy, Rajoelisoa Jeannette from Strasbourg, her husband Rajoelisoa Armandin, and Andrianasolo Jaona from Paris.

A second consecration service was held on October 5, 1980, when three other *mpiandry* were commissioned, one of whom was Dr. Lala.[23] The Toby Pouru St. Remy was also formally recognized as a *toby* associated with the Ankaramalaza revival movement and the MLC. They chose as the dates for their annual meeting July 9–14, because July 14 is Nenilava's birthday. The current *raiamandreny* or "father-and-mother"[24] of the *toby* is Dr. Lala herself, consecrated as such on July 14, 1999.

On May 5, 2002, the first collection was taken for the eventual purchase of land for the *toby*. On December 22, 2005, land was actually purchased for 83,000€ or about $91,000. Architectural plans have been drawn

---

21. Toby Pouru Saint-Remy, "Notre Histoire."
22. *Tobilehibe Ankaramalaza*, 55–57.
23. *Tobilehibe Ankaramalaza*, 57.
24. *Tobilehibe Ankaramalaza*, 58. The term *raiamandreny* ("father and mother") is an honorific used by the Malagasy for any person in authority, from the president of the republic down to the leader of a village community or a parish pastor. The idea is that a good leader *must* have both fatherly and motherly characteristics.

up for the *toby* building, but funds for construction are still being raised at the time of writing.

Nenilava lived in 67 Hectares from the end of 1973 to 1987. The Ambohibao *toby* grew to accommodate a medical clinic in consultation with Sampan-Asa Loterana momba ny Fahasalamana (SALFa), the health department of the MLC. The clinic buildings were completed in 1999,[25] and medical work began in close coordination with the *toby*. Today the work of the Ambohibao Clinic has expanded to include annexes with dispensaries in three other locations within the capital, at 67 Hectares, Anosibe Ifanja, and Tsiroanomandidy.[26] In almost every place where a health center opened, a MLC congregation followed.

Nenilava spent the last period of her life living at the Toby Ambohibao. She rarely traveled during this time except to Ankaramalaza for the annual gathering of the movement and the consecration of new *mpiandry*.

One of the highlights of this part of her life was the consecration, at long last, of a huge church in Ankaramalaza. Nenilava insisted that it had to be built according to the design of a church she had seen in Harstad, Norway. Many different architects were consulted about the building of this structure, but none had succeeded in coming up with a plan that received Nenilava's blessing. She knew they needed a structure large enough to accommodate the massive crowds attending the annual meeting every August. The remoteness of Ankaramalaza, the climate conditions of the east coast rainforest, and the logistics of transporting the building materials across the Matitanana River by small Malagasy *lakana* or log canoes were all quite daunting challenges, beyond the imagination of most architects.

Therefore, Rakotomaro Noel, the president of SALFa, and Stanley Quanbeck, the first general secretary of SALFa, called upon the services of the architectural firm Msaada because of their expertise in working in the developing world. By this time, they had already designed numerous buildings, including clinics, throughout Madagascar. Quanbeck suggested to Andreas Richard, a colleague at SALFa and general secretary of the committee of the Toby Ankaramalaza, that they consider using Msaada for this project, which is how the Ankaramalaza church was finally built.

Nenilava said at the time of the dedication of the Ankaramalaza church that it "constituted the height of her witness to the coming generations."[27]

25. Bertelsen, *Design & Dignity*, 221. See also Agnes, *Ny Tantaran'ny SALFa*, 79, 89.
26. *Diary Trano*, 360.
27. Jaona and Yvonne, "The Prophet Nenilava," 6.

She also said that the church is the "gateway to heaven for many, and it is a treasure above all others for the generations to come. If there is no church [at Ankaramalaza], how will the generations to come remember me?"[28]

All the labor on the church was done by many volunteers and the residents of Ankaramalaza, except for the contribution of Peter Ozolins, the American architect. Andreas Richard said, "This church building is truly built by Malagasy alone."[29] Today the *toby* of Ankaramalaza is home to 424 residents.

The last *toby* founded prior to Nenilava's death was the Toby Fiaferana Ambohijanaka, northeast of Antananarivo. Nenilava first visited the area in 1956, but she returned many times over the years. A young woman from the area by the name of Beby was one of Nenilava's first converts in the early days. Afterwards she lived with Nenilava in Ankaramalaza and became one of her many "spiritual children."[30]

Nenilava continued to visit Fiaferana over the years of her ministry, and by 1988 there were so many converts to the movement that they were able to build a Lutheran church in an area where no Lutherans had ever existed before. In 1989 SALFa opened a clinic in the neighborhood. By 1990 the number of Lutherans in the area and the number of small satellite churches were so numerous that Fiaferana was made an official district of the Synod of Antananarivo. Pentecost 1992 was the last time Nenilava visited in the Fiaferana church. The church later created a *toby* of its own and was officially accepted as such by the *tobilehibe* of Ankaramalaza on June 11, 1994.[31] At the time, though Nenilava lived not too far away in Ambohibao, she was not listed as attending the official dedication of the *toby*. Perhaps she was simply too frail at that time, four years prior to her death.

Nenilava, this great servant of God who gave life to so many both spiritually and literally, died quietly on January 22, 1998, at Ankaramalaza. Eighty years old, she had known for some time that she was dying and asked her spiritual children to take her home to Ankaramalaza so she could end her days there.[32] The news of her death, said her followers, was "like

---

28. *Tobilehibe Ankaramalaza*, 8.
29. *Tobilehibe Ankaramalaza*, 11.
30. *Tobilehibe Ankaramalaza*, 50–51.
31. *Tobilehibe Ankaramalaza*, 52.
32. Personal communication with Rakoto Endor Modeste, June 9, 2020.

being struck by lightening for all of her disciples, but especially so for those who were children of Ankaramalaza."[33]

Rabenorolahy Benjamin, at that time president of the MLC, officiated at Nenilava's funeral service at Ankaramalaza. People came from all over Madagascar as well as from overseas to attend her funeral, including representatives of the Lutheran World Federation and the Norwegian Missionary Society.[34] The prime minister of Madagascar, too, was there, representing the government on behalf of the Malagasy people. This humble woman was posthumously awarded one of the nation's highest honors, *commander de l'ordre national*.[35]

Nenilava was laid to rest behind the Ankaramalaza church, on the eastern side, which is the direction of the ancestors in Malagasy culture and thus the most honored of positions. Yet despite the magnitude of her accomplishments and fame, upon her grave is inscribed only a short text from Philippians 1:21: "For to me to live is Christ and to die is gain," along with her baptismal name Germaine Volohavana, her informal name of Nenilava, her date of birth and death, the timespan of her work from 1941–1998, and the words "Evangelist of the MLC, *Raiamandreny* of the Tobilehibe Ankaramalaza." While this is very fitting to her humble character, so much more could have been written. No doubt, though, her Lord and Savior Jesus Christ greeted her with open arms, saying, "Well done, good and faithful servant" (Matt 25:21).

---

33. Personal communication with Lotera Fabien, November 6, 2020.

34. Why neither the American Lutheran Mission nor the Evangelical Lutheran Church in America were formally represented is not known to me; my family and I had already left Madagascar in 1996, which is why we did not attend. The fact that there was no American church representative is truly to be regretted.

35. There are only a few higher medals than hers, culminating in the Grand Croix de l'ordre national de Premier Classe.

Chapter 3: Interpretation, Analysis, and Appreciation of Nenilava and Her Movement

—James B. Vigen

The story of Nenilava's life would not be complete without telling also of the great influence her witness had on many thousands of people in Madagascar and beyond. This, in turn, has had a huge impact on countless others, rippling outward from person to person across many continents. Besides her personal role in individual people's lives, Nenilava and the Fifohazana movement of Ankaramalaza have played a leading role in the health ministry of the Malagasy Lutheran Church (MLC) as well as shaping the work of NGOs and even politics in Madagascar.

Two of Nenilava's spiritual children and closest confidantes, Andrianasolo Jaona and Randriamanantena Yvonne, wrote an appreciation of her life and ministry after she died. They concluded their study, "The witness Nenilava has left for future generations merits our full attention. She was one of the exceptional men and women who have changed the world, especially the Christian world, with her influence."[1] Readers may hear this as the hyperbole of fandom, but this final section of our study on Nenilava will demonstrate that Nenilava did, indeed, change the world, in the same way that Paul, Peter, and countless other saints of the church have done. Jaona and Yvonne are right to say that the story of Nenilava does, indeed, merit our full attention.

As in this book, so in our analysis, the starting point for studying this great woman is the most authoritative source we have, the only

---

1. Jaona and Yvonne, "The Prophet Nenilava," 43.

"authorized" biography of Nenilava, written in Malagasy by Zakaria Tsivoery, a MLC pastor.

Almost everyone who has written about Nenilava has depended on this short chapter in a larger work on the various revival movements in Madagascar. It is not always clearly recognized that he deserves credit for first putting her story down in print as she herself narrated it to him. Tsivoery's grandson, Ratefinanahary Herimalala Germain, gave me the original manuscript of the work, written down in longhand in simple school notebooks.[2] Examination of the manuscript shows that Tsivoery only rarely made any editorial comment on what he wrote down, nor did he attempt to justify or defend what was told to him except in a very few instances. At the same time, Tsivoery was an enthusiastic supporter of Nenilava and her movement, to such a degree that he was instrumental in the founding of the Toby Nenilava in Fort Dauphin. He does not claim to be an unbiased or even neutral reporter.

And yet, it is striking that Tsivoery did not sugarcoat any part of the story, whether about Nenilava herself or the others in the story, including some of the missionaries with whom she worked. Tsivoery related the occasions when Nenilava herself struggled with spiritual issues, and even when she was rebuked by Jesus. In this respect, her story resonates strongly with the leading figures in Scripture, whose triumphs and failures alike are faithfully reported. A consistent theme in Nenilava's accounts of herself and her work was the rejection of claims of greatness or superiority. She always credited Jesus for the good things that came out of her ministry.

Regrettably, no one has yet written an official follow-up biography to Tsivoery's work, filling in the details of her life both before and after the period that Tsivoery reported on. The principal source available covering Nenilava's later years is a privately published study from 2016, entitled *Tantaran'i Nenilava sy ny Fifohazana ao Madagasikara Boky Voalohany: Soatanana, Ankaramalaza* ("The Story of Nenilava and the Revival Movement in Madagascar"). Author Melchi Razato says that in 1991 Nenilava granted him the authority to write the story of her life while he was living with his family at Ankaramalaza. To date, this book is available only in Malagasy and does not cite or report original sources, as the author himself admits.

---

2. Ratefinanahary confirmed that Tsivoery died in Manambaro Lutheran Hospital on December 1, 1994.

While the previous section of this book completed the biographical account from 1970 to Nenilava's death, more remains to be said about her impact. What follows, then, are stories of some of the notable results and interactions stemming from Nenilava's revival ministry, based on what little written sources exist and also on informants personally known to me through my own eighteen years of ministry in Madagascar. In this I seek to offer an appreciation of her work within the context of a missiological analysis.

Nenilava as Mentor

Lotera Fabien—pastor, professor, director and dean of the Lutheran Graduate School of Theology at Ivory, Fianarantsoa—once wrote, "Nenilava was given a unique gift: she was filled with the Holy Spirit and could read the hearts of people. She was also given all of the different gifts given to the church in Corinth. A few of Nenilava's characteristics: humility—she always sat on a mat on the ground; love—she simply loved everyone; service—she served people all her life; and impartiality."[3]

The aforementioned Andrianasolo Jaona and Randriamanantena Yvonne, a married couple and both *mpiandry* who were consecrated at the Toby Ankaramalaza in the 1980s, list in a study of the Fifohazana movement several major contributions made to the work by Nenilava. With respect to her impact on others, Jaona and Yvonne write, "People felt in [Nenilava] the love of her fellow human beings, whether rich or poor, in her daily life. The exceptional quality of her relations with others was palpable. . . . She was known for her humility. The respect that she accorded to all whom the Lord put in her path reflected that humble attitude that never left her, even in the presence of the least sisters and brothers of Jesus in the Church. . . . Finally, Nenilava was a mother for all of those who knew her. Jesus had promised her many children. . . . Her spiritual children now count in the thousands throughout Madagascar and even throughout the world."[4]

Similar accolades and appreciations could be added by countless numbers of Malagasy, and not only from people in the revival movement. In fact, "during the 90s [every] successive Malagasy head of state came sometimes to consult with her on various delicate affairs."[5] On the only occasion I attended the annual meeting and consecration of *mpiandry* at Ankaramalaza,

---

3. Fabien, "Malagasy Lutheran Church," 3.
4. Jaona and Yvonne, "The Prophet Nenilava," 41–42.
5. Jaona and Yvonne, "The Prophet Nenilava," 42.

in 1995, the president of Madagascar, Zafy Albert, landed the presidential helicopter right on the grounds of the *toby*!

Nenilava was also an immensely important *raiamandreny* to her followers. The word means, literally, "father and mother," and is a figure of central importance in Madagascar. The appellation is applied to every person in authority at every level of society. The president is called a *raiamandreny* to the nation, as are all other government officials over their jurisdictions; heads of departments are called this by their subordinates, and pastors are called the *raiamandreny* of their flocks. The idea is that a good leader will embody the role of both a father *and* a mother: authority figure, protector, provider, as well as nurturer, caregiver, bearer of life. Nenilava was all of these things to her followers, such that it was one of only two roles listed on her tombstone at Ankaramalaza.

Another aspect of Malagasy culture is their veneration of elders and ancestors. Because of this, traditionally Malagasy young people do not chose either vocation or spouse alone without first consulting their literal *raiamandreny* or biological parents. Many people, including many of the most prominent leaders of the Ankaramalaza movement, confessed to me how they broke with tradition and went instead to Nenilava for insight about these all-important life decisions.

So, when young people went to Nenilava for direction about their choice of profession, she would meet with them, discuss the subject with them, and ask them to return in a day or two. Upon their return Nenilava would say, "Jesus wants you to be a doctor" or "a nurse" or "a laboratory technician." Startling though this may sound to the Western mind, the truth is that the MLC's extensive medical ministry simply would not have been possible without the many *mpiandry* who studied for a medical career because Nenilava told them to. When they graduated, almost all of them went to work for the MLC's medical ministry as a way of serving the Lord and his people.

Likewise, Nenilava encouraged many young men to go into the ordained ministry or, in the case of women, to become "female theologians," the term that the MLC uses for women who graduate from the seminaries, since the church does not at present ordain women to the pastorate. Women are, of course, consecrated as *mpiandry*, an office that has grown so greatly in importance in the MLC that by the mid-1980s, when I taught at the main seminary, approximately 95 percent of all seminarians had previously trained as *mpiandry*. It has been suggested that Nenilava directed *mpiandry* toward ordained ministry intentionally in order to secure the close relationship between the church and the revival movement.

Young people also asked Nenilava to show them whom Jesus would choose for their spouse. Here, too, Nenilava would pray over the matter and later inform the petitioner of Jesus' choice. Again, while Western eyes may regard such "arranged" marriages with suspicion, Nenilava's choice would, more often than not, break with tradition by pairing up two people from vastly different people groups and social stations, very much at odds with Malagasy traditional culture. A notable example of this is the case of Rakoto Endor Modeste, former president of the MLC. He came from a prominent Fort Dauphin family, studied at both Luther Seminary in St. Paul, Minnesota, and at the Lutheran School of Theology at Chicago. Nenilava, in prayerful consultation with Jesus, matched him up with one of her own adopted children, Baonizafimanana Jeannette, who like Nenilava herself was largely uneducated. Jeannette once told my wife that she only learned to read from singing hymns in Ankaramalaza! Even more significant than the educational gap was the fact that Jeannette was an Antemoro like Nenilava, while Modeste was an Antanosy. Despite these enormous differences—at least enormous according to traditional Malagasy culture—Jeannette and Modeste forged a successful marriage. They spent Modeste's years of education together in the United States, where Jeannette learned English, preparing her well to become first lady of the MLC! Similar cases of successfully arranged marriages at the direction of Nenilava and Jesus include Lotera Fabien and his wife Soriny Germaine, and Andreas Richard, one of the driving forces behind the MLC's medical ministry, and his wife Rasoanirina Philippine. And this same story could be multiplied by countless other *mpiandry* as well as leaders in the church and nation.

Finally, Nenilava inspired a number of Malagasy pastors and doctors to serve in other countries as part of the South-South Exchange Program. Madagascar provides personnel, while other global partners fund their service in Lutheran churches and hospitals around the world. The South-South program has grown exponentially because of the work of SALFa as well as the large increase in educated clergy, thanks to the expansion in the number of seminaries in Madagascar starting already in the 1980s.

While no statistics have been kept on the subject, the majority of those who have gone out as missionaries from the MLC to other churches have come from the Fifohazana. The MLC created its own mission board, whose mission statement captures well its ecclesiological self-understanding: "The

MLC is an awakened church and preaches the Gospel and carries out revival work (the work of spiritual strengthening) all over the world, especially in lands where there are few Christians."[6]

A good example of this exchange is Mamy Jocelyn Ranaivoson. Mamy worked as a doctor at the SALFa clinic at Ivory, Fianarantsoa, which served both the town and the seminary community. According to Mamy, Nenilava revealed to him that he would become both a doctor and a pastor long before even he thought to imagine such a thing. He was later recruited by Stanley Quanbeck to serve as a South-South missionary doctor in the Evangelical Lutheran Church of Papua New Guinea at Yagaum Hospital on the island of Karkar. While serving there Mamy also engaged in evangelism, putting the revival principles of Madagascar to work in Papua New Guinea. As he described it, "I was the last person that a dying patient would see before they died. I explained that I had done everything [that I could as a doctor] but medicine has its limits. But, remember, God loves you! Jesus died on the cross to save us from our sins. I could see the sparkle in their eyes in thanking me!"[7] After his term of service was over, and because of his experiences evangelizing, Mamy felt called to go to seminary. He graduated from Wartburg Seminary in Dubuque, Iowa, and now serves as pastor at a Lutheran congregation in Onalaska, Wisconsin.

At the time of writing, Malagasy missionaries to other countries numbered thirteen serving in seven different countries. Five pastors, twelve doctors, and one lay person serve in Thailand, Tanzania, Bangladesh, Papua New Guinea, the Comoros Islands, Mauritius, and the Seychelles. One *mpiandry* and doctor named Baozandry worked in Bangladesh for ten years.

Nenilava and Women in Ministry

Nenilava supported and upheld many women individually, but overall her ministry had a profound impact in raising the status of all women in the church. It is not true to say, as some have suggested, that before Nenilava the MLC was indifferent toward women's education. The fact that the MLC does not ordain women is taken as sufficient explanation for this inference, but it is misleading. From the earliest days of theological education in the MLC, the wives of the seminarians were also required to study in their own women's department, in recognition of the fact that a pastor's

---

6. *Diary Trano*, 157.

7. Personal communication with Mamy Jocelyn Ranaivoson, September 28, 2020.

wife inevitably served and was seen as a *raiamandreny* in the parish. Many such seminarians' wives arrived at seminary illiterate, but they didn't leave that way. And not only literacy was taught but also Bible, church history, dogmatics, sewing and knitting (lucrative skills to help support the family), health, and hygiene. All these things raised the status of women immeasurably in church and the wider community.[8]

Nenilava did, however, push the church to go further in providing leadership roles for women. As noted above, she encouraged young people to go to seminary or into other vocations where they could help their nation and its people. The office of the *mpiandry*—which is granted to men and women alike in the MLC—is itself a provocative test case in the doctrine of ministry. A highly developed two-year training program that always takes place under the direction of one or several pastors, it culminates in a ritual consecration that carries official ecclesiastical status. At every jubilee celebration, ordination, or high church festival when the clergy are garbed in their white pastoral robes, the *mpiandry* also are always invited to dress in their own distinctive white robes. More women serve as *mpiandry* than men and in fact do most of the spiritual work of the Fifohazana.

Thus, although women are not presently ordained into the pastorate, the MLC nevertheless recognizes their service as theologians, teachers, and elders of the church. Female elders, for example, may serve as the *raiamandreny* of a particular *toby*. The regional synods are encouraged to give such women paid positions in the work of the synod, and most have done so. I taught some of the first female students coming to seminary in their own right (rather than as spouses). One seminary graduate became the chaplain of the Seaman's Mission at Toamasina, a position she has held for some thirty years. Another became librarian at the Lutheran Graduate School of Theology. And another, Toromaree Mananato, was recently elected as the vice-general secretary of the MLC. She is recognized in the church directory as a *teolojiana* or theologian. The strong leadership role exercised by Nenilava helped pave the way for these younger women to take on more public roles in church and to be acknowledged in turn by the MLC.

---

8. As Richard Shaull wrote in his foreword to Paulo Freire's classic work, *The Pedagogy of the Oppressed*, "those who, in learning to read and write, come to a new awareness of selfhood and begin to look critically at the social situation in which they find themselves, often take the initiative in acting to transform the society that has denied them this opportunity of participation. Education is once again a subversive force." Shaull, Foreword, 9.

Nenilava and Missionaries

Nenilava always tried to work in close consultation with the leaders of the MLC, both Malagasy pastors and foreign missionaries. She always sought to keep the revival movement within the church, not separate from it, but throughout her ministry she had opponents right alongside the supporters within the missionary community. Over time, however, she won over most of her missionary colleagues, who came to recognize her value in the life of the church and nation.

Such words of appreciation, for instance, come from Kjetil Aano, one-time general secretary of the Norwegian Missionary Society (NMS), assistant professor at the School of Mission and Theology in Stavanger, Norway, and missionary in Madagascar from 1979 to 1988. He wrote of how Nenilava "fascinated the Norwegian missionary community more than any other Malagasy individual during the last half of the twentieth century."[9] Aano found a published reference to Nenilava going back as far as 1953, in a story published in the NMS's *Missionstidende*, entitled, "We Have Had an Envoy from Jesus in Our House." Summarizing the article, Aano writes, "The missionary family related how this visitor from the east coast, who had stayed with them for several days, had been a blessing in their lives and had shown them love and a Jesus-like way of living, so that she had left them profoundly touched."[10]

At the same time, as Hans Austnaberg, another NMS missionary who also served in Madagascar and wrote on the Fifohazana, points out, even missionaries who worked closely with Nenilava and were generally supportive could also be critical. Austnaberg quotes at some length another NMS missionary, G. A. Meling, who knew Nenilava personally for about thirty years and worked closely with her on an almost daily basis for about a decade. Meling warned, writes Austnaberg, that "people invent the most incredible stories about her, like journeys to heaven and other miracles. He refers to a pastor from the high plateau who has written an entire book about all the supernatural happenings around Nenilava. Most of this is 'hardly more than overwrought and uncritical verbosity,' according to Meling. Nenilava

---

9. Aano, "The Missions and the Fifohazana," 60.

10. Aano, "The Missions and the Fifohazana," 60. Aano is evidently speaking here of his in-laws. In a footnote in this same article, he mentions that in the 1950s and 60s his wife's parents were missionaries in Vohipeno, the town closest to Nenilava's village of Ankaramalaza, and that his wife knew Nenilava from her early childhood. See Aano, "The Missions and the Fifohazana," 74n36.

herself was little fond of all the talk about her."[11] My best guess is that the critique is addressed against Rajosefa Danielson, a pastor who wrote a book entitled "The Awakening of the Spirit Here in Madagascar," but there is no clear record of who exactly he meant.[12]

The American Lutheran missionaries, on the other hand, were mostly ambivalent about Nenilava in the early years for the simple reason that her work was predominantly in central Madagascar, while the Americans worked mainly in the south. Nonetheless, some American pastors were quite supportive of her, such as Oliver Carlson, Olaf Torvik, and Leonard Jacobsen. After Nenilava came to Fort Dauphin and worked in many of the districts of the southeast, American missionary support for her grew.

Still, one of Nenilava's fiercest missionary critics in the early days of the revival was Vernon Toso, a pastor with the American Lutheran mission. In a circular letter to his fellow missionaries, written in 1967 in his capacity as the Acting Chairman of the American Missionary Association, Toso strongly warned against the Fifohazana movement on the grounds that it violated Article XIV of the Augsburg Confession's assertion that "no one should teach in the church or administer the sacraments, unless he be regularly called."[13] Toso worried that the revivalists' practice of "strengthening" and laying-on hands seemed to place the shepherds of the movement in a higher office than that of the regular ordained clergy—after all, the laying-on of hands has traditionally been the sign of ordination conveyed from one pastor to another. Toso continued in his circular, "The Awakeners' ministry has not been afraid to use the rite of laying-on of hands. It remains a question how much they are satisfying the heathen interpretations and how much they are strengthening the individual Christian's faith. The disturbing part is that they assume the power of the ordained office, fail to see it as a preparation for the main strengthening—the communion service, but have made of it a sacrament of supreme power."[14]

A more nuanced view of Nenilava and the Fifohazana was expressed by Carl L. Ulrich, another missionary pastor, in a paper written in 1972 or 1973 for a master's degree at Luther Seminary in St. Paul. As Ulrich reported, Nenilava and the ministry centered in Ankaramalaza have

11. Quoted in Austnaberg, *Shepherds and Demons*, 52–53.
12. Danielson, *Ny Fifohazam-pany eto Madagasikara*, cited in Austnaberg, *Shepherds and Demons*, 52–53.
13. Melanchthon, "The Augsburg Confession," 47.
14. Toso, "Dear Co-Workers," 2.

> provoked a controversy in the Church as to the place of the revival movement within the Church. Some have advocated that it should be suppressed because it isn't consistent with the Lutheran concept of the ministry. They say it is a super ministry over and above the ministry of the Church. Therefore, we as a mission and Church should not recognize the movement as valid and not have anything to do with it. . . . To this writer, we are cutting off our nose to spite our face when we refuse to recognize that this movement is a part of the Church and has a legitimate place within the Church. It would be a tragedy for the Church if these people, many of whom are fine Christians, are forced to leave the Church and become a sect. From this, Dear Lord, spare us![15]

The Lord apparently heard Ulrich's prayer, since most American missionaries ultimately came to the same conclusion as he did, just as most Norwegian missionaries had. As a result, the Fifohazana movement of Ankaramalaza has stayed within the MLC ever since. Although it may sound to a Westerner like an oxymoron, the MLC now even has an official Department of Revival.

A major obstacle in aligning views on these matters is that the Western world has been engaged in the project of demythologizing for over a hundred years, but this is not so in Africa. As African theologian Stephen N. Ezeanya has written, "[F]or the African, the world of spirits is a real world. . . . [I]t has . . . the closest possible relationship with this material world. It is the spiritual beings which actually control the world; indeed, the world is a spiritual arena in which the various categories of spiritual beings display their powers. Mankind, in particular, is entirely dependent upon these spiritual beings."[16]

What Ezeanya says here about Africa is also true for Madagascar. This being so, for Nenilava and the Malagasy there is simply no hard and fast distinction between "this world" and the "other worlds," as in Western thought. All Malagasy, both Christians and non-Christians, believe in a spirit-world of witches, demons, visitations by dead ancestors, and the like. So for Malagasy Christians, biblical reports of demons or Jacob climbing a ladder into heaven are very real, not simply visions or allegories. The Western observer simply has to accept this. I personally dealt with it the same as when offering pastoral care to people with old-age dementia or mental

---

15. Ulrich, "An Examination," 26.
16. Ezeanya, "God, Spirits and the Spirit World," 35–36.

illness: I do not argue about their perception of reality but do my best to address myself to what they claim to experience.

When Nenilava and her supporters were challenged about reports of her journeys to heaven, seeing Jesus face to face, or other supernatural events, they would point to Paul's words in 2 Corinthians 12:1–5:

> I must go on boasting. Though there is nothing to be gained by it, I will go on to visions and revelations of the Lord. I know a man in Christ who fourteen years ago was caught up to the third heaven—whether in the body or out of the body I do not know, God knows. And I know that this man was caught up into paradise—whether in the body or out of the body I do not know, God knows—and he heard things that cannot be told, which man may not utter. On behalf of this man I will boast, but on my own behalf I will not boast, except of my weaknesses.

Whether Nenilava went to heaven in the body or out of the body, I do not know—God knows. What I do know is that she and her people believed it completely, and that was the reality I had to address myself to in my role as missionary and pastor.

Nenilava and the MLC's Medical Ministry

Nenilava was always as concerned about physical as spiritual healing. She did not require advanced theological training to realize that there is often a direct connection between spiritual health and physical health. She said she learned this from Jesus and reading Scripture. Besides personally helping to found three *toby* and inspiring the establishment of the rest, Nenilava had a direct and influential role in the vast expansion of the medical ministry of the MLC.

One of the key figures in this story is Stanley Quanbeck, a third-generation missionary. He was born and raised in Madagascar, and upon graduation from the American School in Fort Dauphin, Quanbeck went to the States to become a doctor and return to Madagascar as a medical missionary. He saw in this the continuation of the work of one of his childhood heroes, John O. Dyrnes, a doctor who began medical work at Manasoa in southwestern Madagascar in 1899 and worked there, with only two furloughs abroad, until he died in service in December 1943.[17]

---

17. *Missionary Album 1926*, 25. See also Burgess, *Lutheran World Missions*, 146.

After Quanbeck qualified as a medical doctor, he returned to Madagascar in August 1965 with his wife Kathie Quanbeck, a registered nurse. Together they served in the newly created church hospital located in Ejeda in southwestern Madagascar.[18] The Quanbecks labored long and hard at Ejeda Hospital. They helped to establish and run a rural children's clinic that specialized in vaccinations and medicines for children to combat the atrocious infant death rate in the area. The clinic didn't just wait for patients to come to the hospital in a state of crisis, but had personnel make regular visits to villages in the surrounding area to weigh children, follow up on their vaccinations, and maintain charts to track their health.

The Quanbecks always had to fight to find funds, medications, and supplies for the hospital and its programs. The inherent challenges became all the more difficult during the "depravities of the Marxist Socialist revolution of 1972–78."[19] In deep frustration with the devastated economy, which made doing their jobs at the hospital almost impossible, in 1978 the Quanbecks resigned from the mission and planned to return to the United States.

When the national leadership of the MLC learned of this, however, they countered with a proposition. Would Quanbeck, instead of leaving Madagascar, consider heading up the brand new Lutheran Department of Health Work, the Sampan-asa Loterana momba ny Fahasalamana (SALFa)? The Quanbecks asked for some time to pray about this change in plans, but eventually they felt it to be what the Lord was calling them to do. SALFa was officially created by the Standing Committee of the General Synod of the MLC during its meeting at Betioky-South in September 1979, with headquarters in Antananarivo near the MLC central office.[20]

At that time, the medical work of the MLC consisted of two hospitals in the former American districts of southern Madagascar—Manambaro Lutheran Hospital, established in 1954, and Ejeda Lutheran Hospital, established in 1966—a clinic in Andranomadio, Antsirabe (1903) and another in Andohalo, Antananarivo (1886), which were staffed and operated by missionaries of the NMS. There were also a couple of leprosariums in Mangarano near Antsirabe (1887) and at Bekoake near Morondava (1902), as well as schools for the deaf and the blind that also

---

18. *Diary Trano*, 229–31.

19. Personal communication with Stanley and Kathie Quanbeck, October 4, 2020. The Quanbecks are currently compiling a memoir and so were able to share with me this portion of the story about their connection with Nenilava.

20. Personal communication with Stanley and Kathie Quanbeck.

were historically connected with the NMS. While these institutions came under the aegis of the MLC when it became an independent church in 1950,[21] all of them were synodically owned and operated. Each tended to find its own financial and staff support from the mission groups that had founded them prior to the formation of the MLC.

With the creation of SALFa, however, all the health institutions were linked together in a national health care system operated by the MLC. One reason, in addition to government fiscal policies, was to end local ecclesiastical meddling in the operation and funds of the healthcare work, such as the Quanbecks had experienced. Another and even more urgent reason, however, was that it had become increasingly difficult to obtain medications, due to the devastating economic and political conditions throughout the country. Even such common and vital drugs as penicillin or chloroquine (for the treatment of malaria) were no longer being imported by pharmacies in Madagascar on account of the difficulties in foreign currency exchange produced by the policies of the Didier Ratsiraka administration.[22] Therefore, it was imperative to have a central depot for imported drugs as well as a national organization that could seek grants and philanthropic assistance while providing the necessary paperwork and transparency to keep the funds coming.

After the MLC formally constituted the health department, in October 1979 the Quanbecks and their twin daughters packed up and moved to Antananarivo, while the two older children continued on at a boarding school in Kenya. Housing was provided for the family at the NMS compound in the Isoraka neighborhood of the capital. It was a one-bedroom efficiency flat with a single bunk bed and a toilet in the hallway. It became not only their living space but also a temporary office for the secretary general of the MLC Health Department.[23]

---

21. Agnes, *Ny Tantaran'ny SALFa*, 20–56, and Vigen, *Diakonia*, 46.

22. "Madagascar struggled with a crisis of poverty and international debt that [Ratsiraka's] strategies proved incapable of resolving. In the end, these imperatives required a progressive abandonment of socialism and a reluctant but inevitable *rapprochement* with the West." Allen and Covell, *Historical Dictionary of Madagascar*, 256.

23. Personal communication with Stanley and Kathie Quanbeck. After some years of living in these cramped quarters, the American Lutheran Church built a new structure on the Isoraka compound which served as an apartment for the Quanbecks, an office for the SALFa director, and a number of guest apartments for missionaries staying in the capital and visitors. American missionaries had preference in this place, but those of other missions were also welcome on a space-available basis. Members of the "missionary family" could also stay there when "coming home" to Madagascar from retirement,

Quanbeck later admitted to feeling completely overwhelmed by the enormity of the challenge: to seek new and reliable sources of medicines, to secure ongoing financial support through grants and keep them coming, and to find qualified medical personnel willing to work in the MLC health centers, where the pay would be much less than in government service or private enterprise. Above all there loomed the task of expanding the MLC's medical work into other areas of the country, especially where Lutherans had never worked previously, that saw swift growth and were forming new synods of the MLC.[24]

It is at this rather desperate point that Nenilava reenters our story. While the Quanbecks were still settling into their tiny new apartment, on the very first night of their arrival, there came was a knock at the door. Quanbeck recalls, "Opening the door, we were greeted by two young men who introduced themselves as having been sent by the evangelist Nenilava, who told them that Jesus had told her that they should go to Isoraka and inform Dr. Quanbeck that he needs help as general secretary of SALFa. Though we had heard of Nenilava over the years, we had never met her in person; but, quickly did I agree, 'Indeed, I need help,' as I had no idea of where to turn nor what step to take next!"[25]

Thus began a close partnership between Andreas Richard, one of Nenilava's adopted children, which was to last for some twenty-five years. Andreas, at the time an employee of the Malagasy pension program, began to work with Quanbeck in a volunteer capacity, but later he left his government position to work full time for the church and its health department as treasurer. Andreas continued at SALFa until 2010. The

---

as could missionary children seeking their "roots." Today, this structure is operated as a guest house and restaurant by the MLC.

24. When the age of mission control was over and indigenous and autonomous churches were finally in charge, they canceled the longstanding comity agreements on the grounds that they were all now national churches and thus at liberty to go wherever they felt led by the Spirit. This decision has been taken advantage of by the MLC more than other church bodies. One reason for this is that people from the extreme southern part of Madagascar were actively recruited by companies during the colonial period and transported to many other parts of the island to work on plantations. While retaining their clan and tribal connections, they settled down in the areas where they had been transported to work. If they had grown up as Lutherans in their home regions, they longed to continue to be a part of a Lutheran church, and so new congregations sprang up.

25. Personal communication with Stanley and Kathie Quanbeck.

Quanbecks left SALFa leadership in 1999 and retired fully from missionary service in 2004.[26]

The two men together made a powerful combination. Quanbeck had the necessary medical and public health experience, while Andreas had financial and accounting skills but also, perhaps even more importantly, the ability to smooth over conflicts, especially as SALFa grew and expanded its reach considerably over the years and across Madagascar. Again in Quanbeck's own words,

> Mr. Andreas was, by nature, a gifted politician, thus good at settling disagreements, many of which the Lord used him to help tackle, as we were constantly in various conflicts within the church and, occasionally, outside. I, on the other hand, did not have these qualities. So, it seemed, the Lord had paired us, as I repeatedly seemed to have found myself stirring up conflicts which the Lord worked through Mr. Andreas to dampen down. He was a good speaker, the Aaron of our Moses and Aaron relationship, since I, like Moses, felt I "spoke with faltering lips" (Exodus 6:30).[27]

One of Quanbeck's biggest worries about his new position at SALFa was the fact that his rather sparse job description mentioned that part of the department's responsibility was to oversee health issues, sanitation problems, and care of the sick at all of the *tobys* of the church! Quanbeck wondered how he could possibly bring such an enormous mandate to fruition. Here again, Andreas as a *zanaky ny Fifohazana* or "child of the revival" helped pave the way. He arranged for the Quanbecks to visit Nenilava at Ankaramalaza. During their meeting, Quanbeck asked Nenilava "if she would allow us to use modern medicine in her *toby* of Ankaramalaza. Without any hesitation she responded, saying, 'By all means, please do so.'"[28]

This decision turned out to be very good not only for SALFa but for the Fifohazana overall. It was good for SALFa because most *tobys* are located in the rural areas of Madagascar, so by working with the *tobys* SALFa had a ready-made rural healthcare outpost in place. In fact, several *tobys* would later become full-fledged medical clinics working hand in glove with the *mpifohas* or revivalists of the various *tobys*. The move was beneficial to the Fifohazana as well, because one of the major complaints against them

---

26. Agnes, *Ny Tantaran'ny SALFa*, 93; and personal communication with Stanley and Kathie Quanbeck.
27. Personal communication with Stanley and Kathie Quanbeck.
28. Personal communication with Stanley and Kathie Quanbeck.

by Westerners and some missionaries was that the *mpiandry* tended to categorize all aberrant behavior as demon possession without even considering the possibility of mental illness like schizophrenia or medical diagnoses like tuberculosis or leprosy. But as the partnership between SALFa workers and the *mpiandry* at the *tobys* grew closer, a kind of détente developed between them. They mutually agreed that, if a medical cause was suspected in someone who'd come to the *toby* for relief, then the *mpiandry* would first refer the individual to the SALFa medical staff, hospital, or clinic for treatment. If and when the problem was confirmed as having a medical basis, then after treatment the patient would be encouraged to return to the *toby* for supplemental spiritual intervention, especially in cases where a holistic approach to healing seemed most fitting.

The need for this symbiotic relationship was highlighted when a representative of one of SALFa's funding agencies came to Madagascar for an evaluation of the projects, which her organization was supporting. She was taken to Ankaramalaza and given a comprehensive tour of the *toby* and its ministries. She was horrified when she saw a patient at the *toby* physically restrained by chains to a post in the home of one of the *mpiandry*. When she demanded an explanation, the *mpiandry* explained how violent some of the residents could become, in particular those suffering from mental illness; they posed a danger both to themselves and to the *mpiandry* hosts with whom they lived. Such persons had been known to throw themselves into fire, drown themselves, run away into the forest, or physically attack their hosts in the *toby*. It was further explained that the family members who brought the patients for help knew about and consented to the methods of care given at the *toby*. If the patients were calm, they'd be released from the chains and accompany their hosts to church meetings, social activities, and work projects. But when they were violent or self-destructive, the chains were the only means of restraint available.

It is perhaps not surprising to learn that the representative was not at all mollified by these explanations. She returned to her agency and wrote up a report detailing what she called the "human rights abuses at the *toby*." Needless to say, this accusation caused SALFa no small amount of trouble with this and other donor agencies.[29] Quanbeck notes that

> in 1978 the Malagasy Lutheran Church leaders implored the missionary leader of its health department [i.e., Quanbeck himself]

---

29. Personal communication with Stanley and Kathie Quanbeck, and my own personal experience at the time of the event.

to become involved in these mental/spiritual/physical care camps where leaders said even basic standards of acceptable sanitary conditions were not met. Thus began a search for means whereby sensitization concerning primary sanitary and nutrition needs could be facilitated. Through this work, it was soon noticed that the use of chains as physical restrains for violent, agitated, wandering, or possessed patients was quite common. The more that health department personnel worked with the shepherds or caregivers [*mpiandry*] who cared for the ill without any remuneration (solely through love), the more these personnel heard the pleas of the *mpiandry* for help to handle violent, destructive, and agitated patients sent to these *toby* by families who also did not know how to cope with such symptoms in their own homes or villages.[30]

The problem was studied for a long time by SALFa personnel. Discussions were also held with the leadership of the various *tobys*. Finally in 1988 SALFa had devised a plan "to use neuroleptic medication in *toby* patients whom a physician diagnosed as having psychosis or schizophrenia (presence of hallucinations or delusions, out of touch with reality). Theoretically, then, the neuroleptic would be a chemical restraint to replace the chains used as physical restraints."[31] The plan started at the Ankaramalaza and Ambohipinoana *toby*[32] and, having seen great success with the treatment, the program was subsequently expanded to other *toby* as well.

In order to further improve upon the coordination between SALFa health workers and the Fifohazana, a seminar was carried out at Ankaramalaza on July 2–6, 1990, with the ambitious title: "Spiritual healing/oppression (and possession) syndromes/diagnosis of mental illness and the interplay between psychiatric illnesses and demonic oppression, also demonization." William Wilson came from the United States to assist in the training. A renowned psychiatrist and former Duke University professor with expertise in the treatment of mentally ill patients, he also brought to the effort an appreciation of the holistic approach, including a spiritual dimension in the care of patients. In attendance at the seminar was at least one physician from most of the nineteen medical health centers of SALFa at that time. The Ankaramalaza and Ambohipinoana *toby* clinics, where the initial studies had been carried out, each sent two physicians to the seminar.

30. Personal communication with Stanley and Kathie Quanbeck.
31. Personal communication with Stanley and Kathie Quanbeck.
32. *Lisitry ny Toby*, 1. This *toby* is located in the seaport town of Vangaindrano, a former station of the NMS East Madagascar mission.

In addition, there was a social worker, the head of the government medical inspector from the Manakara district, Andreas Richard, and the Quanbecks. The seminars proved to be very valuable training for all involved.[33]

In June 1987 the building at the Toby Ambohibao was completed, and Nenilava made it her primary residence, turning over her former residence at 67 Hectares for use of the church.[34] Upon moving in, Nenilava commented that "this place is not for me only. God has created it for the generations which will follow after forever. I am only passing through here!"[35]

Nenilava and Church Architecture

As SALFa began to expand beyond the number of healthcare centers that existed before its own creation, it was quickly realized that assistance was needed in the building of new facilities. Quanbeck became aware of a new architectural firm that had just started in 1980, Msaada Architects, headquartered in Minneapolis, Minnesota. It was founded by Poul Bertelsen, a Danish architect who had spent eight years in Tanzania working on projects for the Evangelical Lutheran Church in Tanzania—hence the name "Msaada," which is Swahili for "assistance." After moving to the United States with his family, Bertelsen founded Msaada with the express intention of assisting churches and other non-governmental agencies in the global South on a non-profit basis.

SALFa became one of Msaada's first clients. As Quanbeck explains, "The MLC health department accomplished many building projects with Msaada's invaluable assistance, [which] kept us from overstepping our budgetary constraints, kept us in line with standards of building construction, allowed us to negotiate realistically with contractors, [and made possible] the design of appropriate structures for the varied climate . . . [and included] provision of sketches submitted to potential donor agencies, supervision of the construction in progress, and provision of building materials during the lean years of the Marxist Socialist Government."[36]

Soon after setting up an office in Antananarivo, Msaada was invited to complete the long-unfinished church at 67 Hectares. The designs for the building had been drawn up in Norway without consideration for

---

33. Personal communication with Stanley and Kathie Quanbeck.
34. Personal communication with Rakoto Endor Modeste, June 9, 2020.
35. *Tobilehibe Ankaramalaza*, 29.
36. Bertelsen, *Design & Dignity*, 208.

climatic conditions in Madagascar. When this was realized, the building project was put on hold, and the congregation worshipped in a largely unfinished shell of a building for many years. Msaada stepped in and completed the project quickly, including the distinctive church tower that dominates the neighborhood.

When that project was completed, Ankaramalaza leaders asked Msaada architect Peter Ozolins to examine their location and see if he could oversee the design that Nenilava had in mind for the revival center's church. More to the point, they needed to know if it would be possible to get the necessary materials across the Matitanana River, since the other side of the Ankaramalaza peninsula was covered in dense tropical forest without any roads.

Peter Ozolins made the trip to Ankaramalaza and determined that it could be done. He drew up plans that were, in turn, approved by Nenilava. The completed church building—built to accommodate 850 people at a normal Sunday service—was dedicated on August 2, 1995. But at the annual gathering when *mpiandry* are consecrated, the building expands to accommodate a thousand extra worshippers through "the use of fabric 'sails' which create a tented forecourt. The steeple doubles as a support for the sails, while the pillars surrounding the courtyard create a sense of enclosure and demarcate a gathering place even when not used for anchoring the sails."[37] Notably, Ozolins was the only foreigner engaged on the building project; otherwise it was also local labor hired to do the work.

Nenilava and Malagasy Politics

While Nenilava was a prophet and an evangelist of the church, she was not of the stripe that is concerned only with "pie in the sky in the sweet by-and-by." She was a woman who loved her country deeply and asked her disciples to pray daily for the life of the nation, its leaders, and its people. And so it was that Nenilava also involved herself in the politics of the nation.

The anticolonial armed resistance after World War II that took place in China, Algeria, and Vietnam are well known. Less well known is the fact that Madagascar had its own anticolonial insurrection. There was a violent armed uprising against French rule in the island in 1947. It was led by a number of Malagasy who had been quite impressed by none other than Ho

---

37. Msaada Architects, "Lutheran Church for the Toby," para. 1.

Chi Minh, whom they'd met in France.[38] Anticolonial protests and boycotts were held in Antananarivo and many other large cities. The heart of the armed uprising, however, took place on the east coast of Madagascar, near to where Nenilava lived at Ankaramalaza.

The French colonial government had always been quite suspicious of Protestants, since so many of them were English and, in the early years, did not speak French. There was even a popular proverb: *Qui dit Français dit catholique, qui dit Anglais dit protestant*—"Whoever says French, says Catholic; whoever says English, says Protestant."[39] The result of this attitude being fully ingrained into the subconscious of many colonial and military actors, Protestant missionaries and catechists were immediately suspected as instigators of the 1947 uprising. Clergy and teachers in Protestant schools were routinely rounded up and interrogated; many were imprisoned and tried; and of these, many were indicted and exiled or imprisoned.

When I first came to work in Madagascar in 1978, I met a retired synod president named Gilbert Tahilo. Upon learning that I was an American missionary—or whenever the topic of my colleagues came up—he would recount how, during his own arrest and imprisonment during 1947 and 1948, it was the American missionaries who constantly brought him food and books and advocated for his release. He was, he said, forever grateful to them for this witness and support.[40]

Though the French officials were quite biased, they were not entirely wrong in their suspicions.[41] At least one of the main leaders of the uprising put on trial was Monja Jaona, who had, previous to his political involvement, been a catechist in the American Lutheran mission. Almost all the

---

38. "Rapports des deputes avec Ho Chi Minh," 335–37.

39. Cited in Daughton, *An Empire Divided*, 167. See also *La Liberté Religeuse à Madagascar*, 10; Tronchon and Vigen, "Dynamisme ecclesial et affrontements (1896–1913)," 328, where we observe, "Comme beaucoup de generalizations, cette affirmation simplificatrice contient une part de vérité" (Like many generalizations, this simplistic affirmation contains a portion of the truth).

40. Gilbert Tahilo's story was made into a movie by the Board of Foreign Missions of the American Lutheran Church. Missionaries serving in Madagascar played the roles of both missionaries attending to him and the roles of French colonial and military figures. Tahilo played himself as an older man, though younger Malagasy played him as a youth and then as a young pastor falsely arrested and imprisoned.

41. One of the best writings on French colonial attitudes is Mannoni, *Prospero and Caliban*, first published in French in 1950.

others had been trained in Protestant mission schools, though these were neither catechists or pastors.[42]

There is little doubt that most Protestants were likewise biased in favor of restoring Madagascar's independence. But few if any clergy or church workers were participants in the actual uprising. Their sympathy arose not only from nationalist feelings but also because of historical antipathy to the French for their fierce anti-Protestant actions in the early years of the colony. For example, the early colonial French shut down church schools and made it difficult to get permission to build new churches or enter previously unevangelized areas. They forbade the use of church buildings for education, a common practice in most mission fields. These policies had a devastating impact on the social advancement of the coastal and sparsely populated areas.[43]

Despite her vocation as an evangelist and revival leader, Nenilava was no quietist when it came to taking sides in the 1947 rebellion. While the story has been largely ignored by others who have written about Nenilava, a recent publication tells how Nenilava, at great risk to herself, went out alone at night to warn several pastors that they were in danger of arrest and brought them to Ankaramalaza to hide them from the authorities.[44] In Vohipeno, the town closest to Ankaramalaza, there were at the time six Malagasy pastors, forty-eight catechists, and four church-run schools.[45] Nenilava could not save them all, but she did rescue three pastors and their families and led them back to Ankaramalaza to save them from arrest and interrogation and, possibly, death. Nenilava later said of this incident, "It was night when I went at that time, but Jesus was our light."[46]

Statistics regarding the number of people killed by the French in and around Ankaramalaza vary widely. Melchi Razato puts the number at between 89,000 and 100,000 people, while official French government statistics

---

42. See the "notices biographiques" regarding Monja Jaona in Tronchon, *L'insurrection*, 209. Tronchon gives the biographies of twelve main actors in the trials that resulted from the 1947 uprising. Of these twelve, only one is a pastor, though two studied for a time at seminary. Two of the biographies do not list a religious affiliation for the actors, but of the others, two were Roman Catholic, three from an LMS background, two Lutherans, and one each for the Anglican and the French Protestant missions. See Tronchon, *L'insurrection*, 207–17.

43. I describe the story more fully in Vigen, "A Historical and Missiological Account."

44. Razato, *Tantaran'i Nenilava*, 121.

45. Razato, *Tantaran'i Nenilava*, 122.

46. Razato, *Tantaran'i Nenilava*, 125.

admit to 11,200.⁴⁷ Razato's estimation, like that of other scholars, represents not only the ones killed outright but also those who died in the forests from hunger, disease, and wounds. Of the other pastors in the Vohipeno district whom Nenilava could not reach, two were killed and one was thrown into prison and left there for eight months before he was released.⁴⁸

After independence, Nenilava and the Fifohazana returned to their emphasis on evangelization, teaching, strengthening, and the casting out of demons. However, during the presidency of Didier Ratsiraka, a self-proclaimed African Socialist—who was in fact a Soviet protégé with a contingent of North Koreans among his personal bodyguards—the Fifohazana joined with the Christian Council of Churches in Madagascar to oppose his reign. Indeed, when Ratsiraka was finally forced from office by a coup d'état in March 2009, leaders from the Fifohazana were called in to exorcise the presidential palace of all evil elements within it!

Ever since then, the Fifohazana has played a major role in political movements in Madagascar, though sometimes different factions within the movement have stood on different sides of a dispute. Scholars Hilde Nielsen and Karina Hestad Skeie have suggested that the Fifohazana "contributes to both strengthening and expanding the Malagasy worldview. This is why the Fifohazana have become a major site, although not the sole site, for the (re)production of contemporary political imagination, taking account of the dynamics of power and the moral cosmology connected to it."⁴⁹ The Fifohazana of Madagascar thus plays a role analogous to that of African Independent Churches across Africa. The most significant difference, however, is that the Fifohazana remains part and parcel of the historic mission church from which it arose.

Interpreting Nenilava for a Western Audience

Nenilava's impact is extraordinary and inspirational, but aspects of the story are also inevitably disturbing to Christians raised in Western contexts. Although some of these have already been treated, what follows here is a closer look at some of the more difficult aspects of her story.

---

47. Tronchon, *L'insurrection*, 71.

48. Tronchon, *L'insurrection*, 124–25. Two of the pastors Nenilava rescued were from the Vohipeno church, the other from Andemaka.

49. Nielssen and Skeie, "Christian Revivalism and Political Imagination," 218.

Western readers may well be put off by the Fifohazana's lack of interest in the hermeneutics of the historical-critical method or the project of demythologization, as seen in the unquestioning embrace of practices like faith healing and exorcism. It is well worth considering, however, that the *Sitz im Leben* of many Malagasy is much closer to that of the time and place of Christ than to that of North America or Europe in the twenty-first century. The most highly educated Malagasy experience and believe in the spirit world all around them. When they read about Jesus casting out demons in the New Testament, they have no reason to demythologize! Instead, they seek a response from God to their circumstances that will be both effective and protective.

This is exactly what the Fifohazana movement has provided and is the main reason for its great success among the Malagasy people. Lotera Fabien explains, "We are *still* a Lutheran church. For us, the healing ministry is also apostolic. It is a scriptural-based ministry. This specific ministry is somewhat missing in the liturgy of the Lutheran churches in the West and in other parts of the world. Due to scientific assumptions most Western missionaries do not cast out demons, but we believe that God gave the Malagasy Lutheran Church this special gift so that we could confront our traditional and ancestral religions."[50]

Another Malagasy commentator of the Reformed tradition, Laurent W. Ramambason, analyzes the Malagasy situation thus: "[I]t can be said that *mpiandry* emerged 'from above' in reaction to Western and traditional ministerial powerlessness. *Mpiandry* emerged not because classical missionaries or their offshoots, church ministers, betrayed the gospel. *Mpiandry* did not arise, either, without continuity with classical missionaries and church ministers. They did so because the pastorate in its Western form and Malagasy traditional healers could not cope with some of the core problems of the new situation. It was not they as persons who betrayed the gospel: it was rather the scope and potentiality of their ministry."[51]

Ramambason's point is that Western missionaries were not capable of dealing with the Malagasy cosmology that accepts the existence of a spirit-world actively engaged with humankind. When Malagasy Christians read in their Bibles about Jesus and his disciples dealing with demons and possession, they take it quite literally. Western-trained clergy

---

50. Fabien, "Healing Ministry of Ankaramalaza," 6.
51. Ramambason, *Missiology*, 79.

are predisposed to demythologize and therefore do not generally take the struggle against evil spirits seriously.

The Ankaramalaza revival has seen remarkable growth in regions that were not historically assigned as Lutheran mission fields, and everywhere a Lutheran medical facility was established, a Lutheran church emerged soon, too. The MLC made the conscious decision to support the work of the revival and welcomed *mpiandry* into its seminaries, swelling the ranks of clergy who are also *mpiandry*. By point of contrast, this is not the case in the FJKM, Madagascar's large Reformed Protestant denomination, whose theologians have been mostly educated at the Sorbonne in France and so are as thoroughly Westernized as the missionaries. When I worked in Madagascar, I heard many times that an entire FJKM congregation had voted unanimously to secede from the FJKM in order to become a MLC congregation, precisely because of the potent relevance of the revival and the ministry of the *mpiandry* to address Malagasy spiritual concerns. Needless to say, such secessions were protested vociferously by the national leadership of the FJKM, to which the MLC leadership countered that they did nothing to encourage changes of affiliation. But, for all that, the people had the right to decide for themselves with whom they wished to affiliate and for what reasons.

Like many other Westerners, I, too, had to come to terms with this issue early on in my fraternal service with the MLC. Three authors were particularly helpful to me in this regard, and since they are likely to be of use to other Western readers, I'll share their findings here.

The first was Paul Tillich. As a seminarian, I did an independent study on Tillich in my senior year. While I read through his *Systematic Theology* and other works, I was particularly fond of a collection of sermons entitled *The Boundaries of Our Being*. There I read with surprise an address Tillich gave to the graduating class of 1955 at Union Theological Seminary in New York, based Matthew 10:8, in which Jesus tells his disciples to "heal the sick" and "cast out demons." I commend the entire address to anyone who is struggling with the question of demons and possession but will quote one section of the address here:

> Why have these assertions that were so central at the time the Gospel was first preached lost their significance in our own period? The reason, I believe, lies in the words "healing" and "casting out demons," that have been misunderstood as miracle-healing, based on magic power and magic self-suggestion. There is no doubt that

such phenomena occur. They happen here, and everywhere else in the world. . . . It is an abuse of the name of the Christ to use it as a magic formula. Nevertheless, the words of our text remain valid. They belong to the message of the Christ, and they tell us something that belongs to the Christ as the Christ—the power to conquer the demonic forces that control our lives, mind and body.[52]

Well, I thought, if the great Paul Tillich thinks we should take the question of healing and demon possession seriously and does not simply dismiss it, then I'll do the same!

My next guide was psychologist M. Scott Peck. I had read his *The Road Less Traveled* and so took up another of his books, *People of the Lie: The Hope for Healing Human Evil*. This work turned out to be most helpful to me in my continuing search to understand how to deal with the issue of demons and possession in Madagascar. Again, I cannot hope to do justice to it here, though I would encourage every pastor to read this book. Let me just quote briefly from Peck's own explanation as to why he wrote it:

> We cannot begin to hope to heal human evil until we are able to look at it directly. It is not a pleasant sight. Many observed that my previous book, *The Road Less Traveled*, was a nice book. This is not a nice book. It is about our dark side, and in large part about the very darkest members of our human community—those I frankly judge to be evil. They are not nice people. But, the judgment needs to be made. It is the principal thesis of this work that these specific people—as well as human evil in general—need to be studied scientifically. Not in the abstract. Not just philosophically. But scientifically. And to do that we must be willing to make judgments. The dangers of such judgments will be elaborated at the beginning of the concluding section of the book. But, I ask you for the present to bear in mind that such judgments cannot be made safely unless we begin by judging and healing ourselves. The battle to heal human evil always begins at home. And self-purification will always be our greatest weapon.[53]

Peck proceeds in his book to present numerous case studies of actual patients that he had dealt with that brought him to such conclusions. "People of the Lie" is his term for what the Bible would call "demon possession." He explains in the book that he felt his subject matter would be controversial enough

---

52. Tillich, *The Boundaries of Our Being*, 51.
53. Peck, *People of the Lie*, 10.

without adding on all the "baggage" that goes with a discussion of evil spirits in the academic and the medical worlds!

Like Paul Tillich, Peck doesn't believe in either the red-suited caricature of a demon perching on someone's shoulder and whispering in her ear, or in some fantastical evil creature depicted in horror films. But both men do believe in the reality of evil and its power in and over human beings. What exactly is the ontological nature of this evil, neither man speculates upon. This learning, too, was very helpful to me in dealing with the issue of demons in my ministry in Madagascar in solidarity with the MLC. I am content to lay aside ontological speculation and accept the Malagasy cosmological view for what it is, while for myself leaving the issue in the category of mystery.

My third source of wisdom on this issue came from John V. Taylor, who was the General Secretary of the Church Missionary Society of Great Britain and a former missionary himself. I found two of his works very helpful for my own missionary vocation: *The Primal Vision* and *The Go-Between God: The Holy Spirit and The Christian Mission*. In the first of these, Taylor writes:

> If the servant of the Gospel has entered so far into the primal world-view that he no longer confuses its Light with its darkness, he will see clearly how his Master is the Light of the whole world's light and the Liberator from its every darkness. Christ is supremely relevant to African need, if only that need, and not some imagined [Western] one, is brought to him. . . . [The missionary's] method here will be largely Africa's own — the way of confession, absolution, exorcism and reparation. . . . It is significant . . . that so many of the independent Churches, and also revival movements within the "orthodox" Churches, make great use of confession in one way or another.[54]

The reader will recall that this method of operation is precisely the one followed by Nenilava and her followers. Casting out demons was never done independent of worship, the hearing of God's word, confession, and the laying-on of hands.

In Taylor's much larger second work, which is really a full-blown study of pneumatology, he has a whole chapter on "Pentecostalism and the Supernatural Dimension in a Secular Age." Referring to Walter Hollenweger, a specialist on the global Pentecostal movement, Taylor writes:

---

54. Taylor, *The Primal Vision*, 185–86.

[Hollenweger] believes [Pentecostalism] to be vital for a truly ecumenical Christianity, to "understand Pentecostalism as an expression of New Testament forms of religious belief and practice which might be following a very independent line, but could not be ruled out on *a priori* theological grounds." I want to say categorically that I believe the time has arrived when we must take into account all that is positive in the witness of the Pentecostal movement if we hope to press further forward along any of the various roads of liturgical renewal, inter-faith dialogue, the indigenization of Christianity, experiments in Christian community and group experience, the ministry of healing, especially towards psychotics and addicts, and new approaches to church union.[55]

While Nenilava and the Fifohazana movement exhibit many aspects of Pentecostal practice, they did not seek to separate themselves from the Lutheran church, nor did the Lutheran church reject their impulses toward a ministry of healing and exorcism. For this, both parties should be commended and supported.

Other Western readers may be more disturbed ecclesiolgically by the role and place of the *mpiandry* or "shepherds" within the MLC, which has certainly been a longstanding concern of foreign missionaries. Are the *mpiandry* laypeople or clergy? The MLC does not consider the *mpiandry* to be clergy, at least in the Lutheran sense of being ordained to the ministry of Word and Sacrament. Yet at the same time, the *mpiandry* are clearly not "just" laypeople, either. They have their own special clerical garb worn only when working. At church festivals like ordinations or jubilees, the *mpiandry* also vest and process into and out of the church just behind the ordained pastors. Furthermore, the MLC oversees the training of candidates under the direction of a local pastor and senior *mpiandry* for a period of two years. Only then, if the candidates prove ready and trustworthy, they are consecrated (*fanokanana*), a public rite of blessing and recognition within the context of a worship service. Within a threefold office of ministry framework, *mpiandry* might be considered an order of deacons. Unlike the ordained pastors, however, the *mpiandry* are totally self-funded in their work. Rasolondraibe describes the *mpiandry* as "preacher-healers."[56]

Another aspect of this story may alarm certain Western readers as well, namely the fact that while Nenilava is still almost universally revered and women comprise more than half the number of *mpiandry*, the MLC

---

55. Taylor, *The Go-Between God*, 200–201.
56. Rasolondraibe, "Healing Ministry in Madagascar," 347.

does not ordain women into the pastoral office of Word and Sacrament. I confess that this remains a stumbling block for me. When I taught in Madagascar, I would challenge my students, asking them, "Which is greater in the kingdom of God, a prophet or a pastor?" "A prophet," they would respond without fail. "Was Nenilava a prophet or not?" I would further ask. "Oh, yes, she was a prophet!" they always replied. I would then make the obvious point that if Nenilava, a woman, was called to the higher role of prophet by Jesus himself, why could no other Malagasy women serve in the lower role of pastor? They had no answer to this question.

However, to their credit or at least honesty, the MLC does not proffer scriptural grounds for its refusal to ordain women to the pastoral office. Instead, they frankly admit that the obstacle is cultural. They insist they're simply not ready. But despite their unreadiness, they willingly respect and acknowledge Nenilava as the most important leader of the Fifohazana and how she opened the way for women to serve as both *mpiandry* and *raiamandreny* of a *toby*. Other opportunities for Christian women to serve and to lead will no doubt arise in the years to come.

Nenilava's Lasting Impact

It is beyond dispute that Nenilava had a huge impact on not only the Lutheran but the entire Christian church in Madagascar. When she began her ministry in the postwar period, the major urban centers were well evangelized and served by Christian schools and other institutions. The region of Imerina was overwhelmingly Christian, though many scholars and even Malagasy themselves doubt how deep their faith commitment was. None of this was true, however, in the rural areas of the island. Thanks to the work of the Fifohazana led by Nenilava, great inroads have been made toward the evangelization of the whole of Madagascar. Each *toby* has become an outpost for Christian outreach and service.

Moreover, while Nenilava certainly contributed to the numerical growth of the church, she also served to bring about a true indigenization of the faith among the Malagasy people. Péri Rasolondraibe, a pastor within the Fifohazana with a Western education, has described the role of the movement in fully indigenizing the faith of Malagasy Christians in this way:

> [T]he healing ministry of the revival movement provides both an open window into the tradition of early Christianity (as expressed in the Book of Acts) and an open door into the Malagasy culture

and soul. Healing—mending the broken, caring for the disabled and the old—is a deep-seated habit among the Malagasy; therefore, it must be a part of Malagasy religion. A Christianity which banks only on intellectual piety will not be received among the Malagasy as good news. Early Christian tradition kept the proclamation and the demonstration of the Lordship of Jesus Christ together. The shepherd ministry of Madagascar attempts to maintain that tradition and thus serve the needs of the people. . . . In the theology of the revival movement, God's healing takes place through the hearing of the good news, through the experience of his renewing power, and through his historical acts of liberation and reconciliation of people in communities. God heals, and God empowers people to be instruments of healing.[57]

Rasolondraibe was speaking of the Fifohazana movement in general, but what he has to say applies specifically to Nenilava, who ended up leading the largest contemporary revival movement in Madagascar.

It is clear that Nenilava's influence upon the Fifohazana, her nation, and the whole world has been profound. She helped to transform the face of the ministry in Madagascar, effectuated a deeper indigenization of the gospel, and expanded the church into rural areas thus far unchurched. She provided care for many in need both spiritually and physically, for the mentally ill, for outcasts and many others besides. She upheld the value of each and every human life she encountered.

It is no exaggeration to affirm with the church in Madagascar that Nenilava was a prophet of God and a great servant of Jesus Christ. The Fifohazana movement that she founded and led for so many years continues to serve by following her superlative example.

Concluding Thoughts on Nenilava

Nenilava was obviously a woman of great charisma and exerted a powerful attraction on the people who came into her presence. Her charisma, however, was not that of a glad-handing politician or televangelist. She was, instead, humble and soft-spoken in her dealings with people. The only time she raised her voice was when she preached or spoke out against demonic forces, casting them out during spiritual work (*asa*). Even in those cases, when she raised her voice—as do all *mpiandry* as they cast

---

57. Rasolondraibe, "Healing Ministry in Madagascar," 350.

out demons—it was not in imitation of revivalists from other countries but rather because she and her colleagues believed that Jesus himself had done the same.[58] Lotera Fabien wrote of her, "Nenilava never cast out demons with a quiet voice. She shouted at the demons. She was often heard exclaiming, 'Come out, Satan, in the name of Jesus of Nazareth! Leave this person, they do not belong to you! You steal God's people! Get out in the name of Jesus Christ!'"[59]

While Nenilava is the equal of the great and charismatic leaders of African Independent Churches in terms of her accomplishments and the impact of her work on her country and beyond, she always deflected attention away from herself to point to Jesus and to give him all the credit for any wonderful thing that happened because of her ministry and work. Nenilava's closest followers were called her "spiritual children," and so they, in turn, called her "Mama" or "Mama Neni." Indeed, at the time of her death, three of the main leaders of the Ankaramalaza movement issued a press release about her, which concluded by saying, "If the future [of the] work [should] be grounded on miracles and different visions, it will be demolished. To all of us who continue her work, we should not be filled with worries . . . but be strong and have faith. Mama said: 'If you want to call me Mama, love Jesus.'"[60]

Mamy Jocelyn was, for a number of years, Nenilava's doctor. He writes, "I used to do a medical check-up on her once a week. She told me many stories of her life. She was a very humble person. Jesus spoke to her directly, she said, and prophesied." He testifies that Jesus' prophecies, relayed through Nenilava, came to pass in his own life.[61]

Andrianasolo Jaona and his wife Randriamanantena Yvonne are both members of the MLC, based at Ambohibao, and serve as general secretaries of projects for the Toby Ankaramalaza. This is how they remember Nenilava:

> She was a woman who loved God above all, and feared him. Her passion was to serve him. In her everyday life we could sense the

---

58. In the Malagasy Bible, the word for "rebuke" (from Greek *epitimao*) was translated as *miteny mafy*, "to speak loudly or harshly," there being no Malagasy equivalent for "rebuke."

59. Fabien, "Malagasy Lutheran Church," 5.

60. Press release from Andreas Richard, Rakoto Endor Modeste, and Rabarioelina Bruno. Cf. Austnaberg, *Shepherds and Demons*, 55.

61. Personal communication with Mamy Jocelyn Ranaivoson.

love of neighbor, whether rich or poor. The exceptional quality of her relationship with others was palpable. We knew her, body and soul, to be consecrated to the work of God and to pray for others to come to the knowledge of Jesus. She was also known for her humility. They respect that she devoted to all those whom the Lord put in her path reflected this humble attitude from which she never departed, even in the presence of the least of Jesus' brothers in the church. Practically all her life manifested Jesus, seeing the world through the eyes of his holiness and his love.[62]

From these observations it is clear that what attracted people to Nenilava was not her own personal charisma or magnetism but rather the fact that people saw a reflection of Jesus in her. And that was precisely the way she wanted things to be.

---

62. Personal communication with Andrianasolo Jaona and Randriamanantena Yvonne, "Toby Ankaramalaza—Le Témoignage de Nenilava—Nov. 2007." Translation from the French by JoAnne Albing Vigen.

Conclusion

—Sarah Hinlicky Wilson

By now we have traced the twists and turns of Nenilava's life and ministry and the impact she had on the Malagasy Lutheran Church, the nation of Madagascar, and other points farther abroad. Therefore, it is time to pose that classic Lutheran question: what does this mean?

In what follows I will present an effort at interpreting Nenilava's history for a Western audience, the fruit of my own study and reflection on the issues raised thereby. In so doing, I aim not to resolve or conclude the discernment process but rather to open it up for further engagement among Lutherans and other Christians throughout the world.

Evil Spirits

Perhaps the most immediately startling aspect of Nenilava's story is the ubiquitous presence of evil spirits or demons. Neither Nenilava nor Tsivoery saw any need to defend their experience or perception of evil spirits at work in people's lives, or even to explain such a thing. It is simply taken for granted. Needless to say, this is not the usual approach among Westerners, though it should be noted it is not entirely absent, either.

The question is stark and simple: *what*, exactly, was Nenilava battling against?

To begin answering this question, let me share an anecdote from my first visit to Madagascar.

My family and I were in Ranomafana National Park, following a ranger who tracked down various species of lemurs for us. (So yes, I did get to see the strange and wondrous animals of Madagascar!) Accompanying us on the trip were two young men, students at the Lutheran Graduate

School of Theology as well as *mpiandry*, preparing for ordination as pastors. By this point I was half-convinced and half-skeptical over the whole business of exorcism, so to one of these two I put a barrage of questions as we hiked through the forest. The question I pressed hardest was the one that every Westerner ends up asking: how did they *know* it was an evil spirit and not, say, physical or mental illness?

I should mention that I was not particularly convinced by the modern assumption that all things identified as evil or impure spirits in the Gospel accounts were just mislabeled cases of "natural" illness. The prospect of battling against demons was tolerable to me if it took place two thousand years ago and in the presence of the incarnate God. But right now, and in a place I could reach by airplane, the same prospect strained my credulity.

The student responded to all my questions calmly and thoughtfully. Indeed, he said, part of *mpiandry* training is to distinguish between medical and mental illness, on the one hand, and spiritual affliction, on the other.[1] He talked about the importance of education regarding bilharzia, a waterborne parasite that causes illness in rural areas of Madagascar and can result in bizarre behaviors often mistaken for demonic possession. He told me about reading up on schizophrenia because there were cases where he thought that was the real problem, not demons, and as such required corresponding treatment.

For all that, he maintained, affliction by evil spirits was a separate condition that many of his countrypeople suffered, and it was essential to offer them spiritual release. In particular, he noted, this was due to the continued practice of divination and sorcery among the Malagasy. He described this to me as individuals deliberately inviting evil spirits into themselves in order to acquire power over others, including secret knowledge and the ability to curse. His own grandparents, in fact, had been practitioners of this kind of dark magic. In his experience—and I heard this from other *mpiandry* as well—that kind of willing welcome of evil powers into oneself was not shaken off in a moment but required multiple interventions by the church before the practitioner would be fully set free.

At this point, I was so impressed by the evident care and discernment that undergirded the MLC's exorcism ministry that I felt, to put in plainly, pathetic and embarrassed at the spiritual weakness of the churches I'd known all my life. Grasping at anything to bolster my image, I mentioned to the student

---

1. In fact, the official *mpiandry* handbook stipulates that shepherds "are not permitted to hinder a sick person from going to a doctor." See *Fifohazana Miray*, ch. V, art. 4.

that in Strasbourg (where I was living at the time) there was a charismatic Lutheran congregation whose worship services I attended on occasion, and at times they would engage in singing in the Spirit. I omitted mentioning that, the first time I heard it, I mistook it for jazz scatting and had to be enlightened by my husband as to what was really going on.

But then, to my utter perplexity, this Malagasy student *mpiandry*, who had just spoken at such eloquent length about battling the demons, responded with scoffing disbelief: "What? Tongues? You mean *blah blah blah*? I don't believe in any of that stuff!"

The lesson I took away from this exchange was: plausibility is a culturally contingent matter! And to accept one unusual or provocative "spiritual" reality is not necessarily to accept them all.

So, then, what is a plausible explanation to a Western audience of what Malagasy Christians experience? There is inevitably going to be a gap between the experience and the explanation, and we may as well acknowledge that fact up front. What I'll share here is the explanation that seems most plausible to me.

The first point to make is, as mentioned above, that there was always a gap between what I was willing to believe about scriptural accounts and what I could admit in my own time and place. If I "believe" in evil spirits or admit their existence, it is only because they are assumed in the New Testament narratives. I have never particularly felt the need to demythologize the Bible on this score, but I have equally not felt the need to impose its categories on my present reality. Indeed, I have often been disturbed by the efforts of Christians in Western settings to do so—it has always seemed to me stagey, sensationalistic, and a tool in variously conceived culture wars, rather than an honest encounter with either the God of the gospel or his enemies.

That said, it has become increasingly clear to me that even if Westerners do not name or define "demons" and "evil spirits" as either the Malagasy or the biblical narratives do, we do talk about certain experiences in ways that reveal our own kind of perception of invisible forces beyond our control. These are categorized and explained in a variety of ways: for instance, we speak of mass hysteria, mob mentality, cultural memes, the spirit of the age or your alma mater or a sports team, the unconscious or the subconscious. Readers have no doubt had the experience of waking up in the morning only to feel emotional stormy weather brewing in the air—usually leading to a big fight—or of visiting a house where everything felt sick and wrong.

We may talk about such things as the outworkings of a family system (for example), but you can't *see* or *hold* a family system. It's a metaphor, and a very useful one, for getting a hold on a reality that seems to impose itself on family members quite apart from their volitional consent. Likewise, if you've spent more than ten minutes in any given Christian congregation, you have seen the same thing at work: there are healthy congregations whose "spirit" is lively, faithful, and fruitful, and there are utterly toxic congregations where "evil" is the only language adequate to the situation—see Revelation 2 and 3 and a great deal of 1 Corinthians! But *what* are we actually talking about in these cases? What *is* a "compulsion to repeat" or a "Zeitgeist" or "team spirit"? As Westerners we are most comfortable with metaphors, but the very fact that we resort to using them indicates that we, too, perceive forces for good and for ill beyond our control and desire.

Are these forces, then, evil spirits (or good ones)? Having talked to Malagasy *mpiandry* about these things, I would say for myself that I've moved from being an unbeliever to an agnostic on the issue. I use the latter word deliberately: *I do not know*, and I do not believe I am in a position to judge. I'm not willing to conclude that my fellow Christians in Madagascar are utterly deluded or misled in their spiritual discernment. At the same time I cannot, nor do I wish to, abandon the intellectual development of my own Western culture as if in a heroic act of *sacrificium intellectus*—not least of all because I am well aware of the ways in which belief in evil spirits can itself be dangerous to Christians, who feel thereby authorized to demonize other human beings.

But more to the point, I'm no longer convinced that it is especially helpful to draw any conclusions about the *ontology*—that is to say, the precise nature of the reality, whether spiritually or scientifically construed—of what people experience as "demons" or "evil spirits." I suspect that assertions that demons definitely "do exist," and assertions that they definitely "do not exist," are equally distractions from the Christian ministry and its discernment of spiritual needs, not a confirmation of that ministry either way. From the perspective of the gospel, what advantage would it serve to know for sure that demons "exist"? At most, the reassurance that God fights against them on our behalf; but then, we already knew that God fights against evil for us and for our salvation. To my mind, certainty about demonic "existence" would offer us nothing that we didn't already know.

Allow me to bolster the point with two further observations. First, although the New Testament certainly assumes evil spirits, it displays no curiosity about them whatsoever. There is no speculation as to their origins, ontology, or ultimate prospects. They are simply there, and not for the good of God's human creatures, hence the practice of exorcism.

Second, and related, I have found in other orthodox Christian practices of exorcism a similar lack of curiosity about demons. The most famous Lutheran exorcists are father and son Johann Christoph Blumhardt and Christoph Friedrich Blumhardt,[2] who lived in Germany in the late nineteenth and early twentieth centuries. The elder Blumhardt in particular engaged in an extended battle against spiritual evil afflicting one of his parishioners, Gottliebin Dittus. After nearly two years of Blumhardt's prayer and presence with Dittus, the evil—whatever it was exactly—gave up its hold on her and her siblings, one of whom shouted in the moment of release, "Jesus is Lord!" This became the basis of all of Blumhardt's (and Dittus's) ministry thereafter. But Blumhardt conscientiously eschewed speculation on the powers that held the Dittus family, despite the fact that it was fashionable to do so in the spiritualist atmosphere of the time.

What Blumhardt concluded echoes what Luther also learned in his several forays into exorcism: that calm prayer, invocation of Jesus' name (but not as a mantra or magic word), and the faith of the church and its ministers is more than enough to fight the demons. No study of or preoccupation with what they are or how they work is required to get the job done. If anything, to pursue the topic further is to inveigle oneself afresh in spiritual danger.[3] It is enough for the devil to be renounced at baptism—an aspect of the medieval liturgy that Luther retained, though he did delete the actual exorcism of the infant child.

A final general remark on exorcism in the Malagasy context. Westerners tend to think of exorcism according to the pattern of the famous movie, *The Exorcist*, and other Hollywood (or fringe Christian) depictions of sinister humans who need a solid spiritual whack from a priest to force them to break the alliance. It became clearer to me on my second trip to Madagascar, while attending worship services led by *mpiandry*, that this is not, in general, how the MLC understands its exorcism work. Certainly there are cases of willing collaborators, like former practitioners of sorcery. But overwhelmingly exorcists do not single out possessed people as

---

2. The best studies in English of the two men, respectively, are Ising, *Johann Christoph Blumhardt*, and Zahl, *Pneumatology and Theology*.

3. See, for example, Luther, *Letters of Spiritual Counsel*, 42–45. See also Wengert and Krey, "A June 1546 Exorcism," 71–83, in which the authors note the role of postbaptismal exorcisms of saved but afflicted Christians.

collaborators with evil. Rather, they strike down people's daily experience of affliction by evil of all kinds.

Madagascar is one of the poorest countries in the world, with correspondingly low levels of health, hope, and opportunity. Suffering is the norm, not the exception. Simply to exist is to feel afflicted much of the time by dark and loveless forces. As such, people come to services led by *mpiandry* again and again, not for one-time release from a single demon that directs them like a puppet master, but for continual restoration to God's gracious purposes against all their daily indignities and griefs. The need for and the good of that is, I think, beyond dispute.

Healing and Miracles

Unexpected and inexplicable healing of chronic or fatal illness is not as foreign to Western Christian experience as exorcism, but it is also a neuralgic point of contention. The issue is, however, not so much the *fact* of miraculous healing as its *interpretation*. Two obstacles in particular obstruct a healthy Christian teaching on this topic; I'll address the first in this section, and the second in the next.

The first is the conflict that the West assumes to exist between "science" and "religion." Although this is a false dichotomy, engineered in the collusion between a certain kind of scientific rationalism and a certain kind of responding religious fundamentalism, it still operates as the fallback position even of Westerners who would rather disavow it. This essay is not the place for an extended historical analysis of how science came about specifically as a product of Christian thought patterns, the many ways in which science and Christianity tracked together and interwove through several centuries, or how divergences between the two were politically exploited by both sides. Instead, I will offer here a brief theological critique of its underlying assumption as it plays out with regard to miraculous healing.

The thought structure that lies at the base of the science/religion dichotomy is an equally false nature/supernature dichotomy. This posits, first of all, "nature," which under ordinary circumstances operates according to internal and immutable laws and blindly results in predictable effects. Set aside the fact that this reflects a Newtonian physical universe and not a quantum one; the point is that "nature" here is a self-contained system that needs God at most to set it in motion, but otherwise can grind along just fine on its own. Since this system is self-sufficient and self-enclosed, the only way to posit God's involvement (past the moment of creation) is for God to interfere, interrupt, and invade an optimally functioning system, either to favor one creature arbitrarily over others, or to reveal knowledge that is unavailable to the self-enclosed system of nature. Such interference comes from "supernature" or "the supernatural," which lies "above" nature.

One of many problems with this thought structure is that both suboptimal functioning within nature, and ignorance of supernature, are entirely relative to the figures within the enclosed system of nature. Bluebirds, giraffes, and algae do not suffer from their ignorance of supernature. And a malaria protozoan is quite happy infecting a human being. If God is a just creator, equally concerned for all of his creatures, on what grounds does he prefer one over the other?

As long as this paradigm remains the tacit working assumption, there will be no choice but to be stuck with a pair of false alternatives when unexpected healings come about. *Either* the healing was in fact "natural" and the only problem is that we humans are insufficiently adept at science to perceive the mechanism, therefore God did not cause it and no miracle took place; *or* the only way to honor God's care for his human creatures is to identify in the healing a "supernatural" violation of his own designed laws, therefore any "natural" explanation must be rejected as demoting the glory of God. There is no way around the impasse, so long as these terms of debate are accepted.

Happily, however, the terms of the debate owe far more to the ancient Greek philosophical tradition, and later Enlightenment and Deist reworkings of that heritage, than to the biblical witness. Much of Christian intellectual history has been plundering Greek (and later other cultures') philosophies and conceptualities in order to make the gospel intelligible to members of those cultures, but the price is inevitably paid of tangling up the gospel in accounts of reality that simply don't fit its witness. This is not a problem that can be avoided. It can only be recognized and addressed, again and again, as the gospel continues to wend its way through time and space.

The better and more biblical dichotomy, by contrast, is the one between Creator and creature. Despite a superficial resemblance, this is not the same as the distinction between supernature and nature. In the first place, it does not presume the self-sufficiency and self-enclosure of the created system; quite the contrary, it asserts continual presence and preservation on the part of the Creator, such that the creature always stands in relationship to the Creator. It further rejects the supernature/nature assumption of parallel laws and knowledge, one of which is simply "above" the other and not accessible within the "lower" system without some penetration of the one to the other. Between Creator and creature there is an ontological *chasm*, not an ontological *parallel*. Disorder and ignorance are the consequence of the creature's alienation from the Creator, not the bad luck of being stuck on a lower plane. This, it must be remembered, is a *theological* assertion of faith for faith. To attempt to verify scientifically the problem of sin and death as alienation, for example, is inevitably to fall back into the supernature/nature paradigm.

Moreover, the Creator/creature dichotomy rejects the definition of a miracle as God's intervention into otherwise functional laws for arbitrary if kindly purposes. In order to redefine "miracle," however, we need a further Christian interpretation of the very term "Creator": for gospel faith, this means not the wholly other that set creation in motion long ago and then exited the stage, but rather the one who has continually called his human creatures into fellowship, stayed faithful to them despite their collusion with sin and idols (and demons!), became incarnate within creation in order to do so, rose from the dead on the same earth that he created, and will at the last bring this creation to a new fulfillment. In other words, the Creator/creature dichotomy not only suggests a difference in the Creator's "being" from that of the creation, but also narrates a history between the two through and beyond time. This history is one that does not pine for a pristine past but strains toward an eschatological future. Thus, understood in Christian perspective, miracles are not random suspensions of permanently valid laws, but signs pointing toward a future restoration of all things. It's worth remembering here that no miracle is conclusive—because even healthy and restored bodies eventually come to a temporal end in death. Something is required beyond miracles: the new creation!

In light of this, how ought we to interpret the miraculous healings that attended Nenilava everywhere she went?

Acknowledging the reality of her healing ministry does not require accepting every reported event. For myself, I cannot but take the story of the man whose eyeball hung down out of its socket and later popped back in to be anything other than pious accretion! Vigen also mentions at least one missionary who trusted and admired Nenilava's work but disliked the overwrought tales that tended to spring up around her. Discerning distinctions are not the same as doubt or disbelief.

Nevertheless, it seems clear enough that Nenilava would not have attracted the number of followers she did, nor given birth to a new ministry, nor remained so universally admired, if all the miraculous healings attributed to her intervention were fiction. There is a bedrock of truth in the stories that surround her: Jesus Christ worked powerfully through her, and the result was that many people experienced healing.

I'll take up the question of spiritual healing from sin in the next section, but even in the realm of bodily and mental illness, a great range of healings is attested to during the course of Nenilava's ministry. This should prompt the further reflection that the generic terms "illness" and "healing" cover a great range of issues.

For example, there is infection, as in the aforementioned case of malaria, but malaria is quite different from an infected wound. Both of these are attributable to microscopic organisms that share the earth with us, but that in itself does not make them our enemy. Think of the many microorganisms we depend upon to ferment our bread, cheese, and wine, or the trillions of microorganisms—outnumbering those with our own DNA!—that reside in our bodies, maintain our equilibrium, and protect us from worse intruders. There is injury due to, say, gravity, as in the case of falling, but gravity is the reason objects hold together, so we could not be bodies at all, with or without broken legs, lacking gravity. These illnesses are all byproducts of the very creation of which we are part.

But of course, there is also illness when something goes wrong internal to itself. Consider autoimmune disorder, when our bodies turn on themselves, or cancer, when cells illegitimately aspire to infinite growth and immortality, which left unchecked will kill not only the host but the cancer, too. There is chronic pain of all kinds, from those induced innocuously by a career spent sitting and typing to the phantom pains felt by amputees where their limbs used to be. There can be a distortion in the reproductive transmission of genetic code, in some instances so severe that babies with such genetic defects will not live more than a few hours past birth. There are many more cases of stillbirth and miscarriage for similar reasons. But this also is complicated: other genetic disorders permit a reasonable lifespan. While they may impair physical or intellectual functioning, should every one of these be regarded as "illness"?

And this is just to list what appear to be purely physical illnesses! What then of the variety of mental, emotional, and psychological illnesses? These can stem variously from injury, genetic disorder, chemical imbalance, trauma, social disorder, and deeply entrenched family patterns. There is even emerging epigenetic evidence that experienced harm can be encoded and passed down through the generations physiologically. And some illnesses are now called "diseases of affluence," which in a painful irony expose the mismatch when creatures intended for danger and famine suddenly get more rest and nourishment than they ever could have anticipated. Be careful what you wish for!

A broken bone is pretty easy to diagnose, and an exploding appendix is (nowadays) pretty easy to treat. But the ease of both diagnosis and treatment evaporates rather quickly from there on out. Western medicine has made fantastic advances, especially in the case of acute care, but all too many chronic conditions remain frustratingly resistant to analysis and cure. I suspect that the expanding willingness of Westerners to dabble in all kinds of "alternative" therapies from the almost-mainstream to the extremely marginal is proof of how great the desire for healing is, and how rarely it is found.

The upshot of this roll call of illness is not to undermine confidence in what Western medicine can in fact do well, nor to commend what is derisively called "faith healing" as the cure-all for every disorder. It is rather to emphasize the complexity of our bodies, our minds, the interaction between the two, and the interaction of ourselves with our environment. If this is the case, then it is not surprising that the powerful presence of a woman speaking in Christ's name and with Christ's authority should interrupt some, many, or all of the interacting processes that cause human beings to be physically and mentally unwell.

The critique that such holistic healing points at Western medicine needs to be formulated precisely: because Western science is predicated on isolating and testing single variables, then if a (for instance) health problem is due *not* to a single variable but to the interplay of multiple variables—spiritual, emotional, psychological, physiological, familial, social, environmental, and so on—it very quickly becomes computationally impossible to trace out every possible causal connection and thereby land on an uncontestable cure. What a ministry like Nenilava's can do, by contrast, is address human beings as whole creatures, set in relationship both to God and to other creatures, whose needs, pains, and failings will manifest in a whole host of ways. Is it so strange, after all, that the body-soul-unity-set-in-community that is a human being might manifest its spiritual disorder physically or its physical disorder spiritually?

It's important to remember here that Nenilava was no critic of the introduction of Western medical practices to Madagascar. On the contrary, she welcomed them. The Ankaramalaza revival and its *toby* outposts became crucial players in the extension of medical and mental healthcare throughout the island. The relevant point is that, if one operates with a Creator/creature paradigm rather than a supernature/nature one, there is simply no reason to pit spiritual healing of the kind Nenilava did against scientific healing of the kind that Western medicine does. These are complementary practices, not competitive ones.

In this perspective, then, we can see more clearly the right Christian interpretation of the concept of miracle. A miracle is not a matter of a "supernatural" God abrogating his own otherwise good and reliable laws of "nature" in order to effectuate a biased intervention on behalf of an individual creature, possibly to the detriment of other creatures. What we call miracles are rather the ongoing manifestation of God's preservation of the created order that he made and loves, as well as testimony to his intention to bring it to eschatological fulfillment. Miracles are witnesses to the Creator's character, rather than violations of the Creator's rules. It was for precisely this reason that Luther chided those whose attention got riveted on spectacular recovery but remained unmoved by a person who lived in good health her whole life long.[4] Given the multiplicity of threats to bodily and mental integrity, which is really the more miraculous? Only a bias toward "supernature" prefers a spectacular recovery to lifelong good health.

And yet, even the greatest of healing miracles does not result in the elimination of death. Everybody dies, even those who are preserved a little longer than others. To grapple with death, another factor has to be taken into account: sin.

---

4. "*Nemo in mundo fere, qui gratias deo, quod ein fein zunge, ohr, qui sunt, qui haberuent 50 jar ein fein gesicht, qui ex corde etc. quot sunt, qui sich des grossen wundern freuen? Hic mirantur, quod illum sanavit sed quod ipsi audiunt non est mirum. Per minora illa miracula excitat, ut intelligamus maxima, quia totus mundus est surdus, quia non intelligit.*" (There is nearly no one in the world who would thank God for his fine tongue or ear. There are people who have had a fine face for fifty years, but how many are glad from their heart about this great wonder? Here, they wonder that he healed that man, but that they are able to hear is no wonder for them. Through those smaller wondrous things he challenges us so that we understand the greatest wonder, since the whole world is deaf because it does not understand.) Luther, "Sermon on the 12th Sunday after Trinity," 46,493,22.

Healing and Sin

The faulty paradigm of supernature/nature is the first of the two obstacles to interpreting miraculous healings aright in a Western context. But probably the more urgently felt problem is the way in which healings, or more to the point *non*-healings, are deployed within a religious setting.

It is one thing to rejoice that a beloved friend has been rescued from the brink of death by means beyond the explanatory power of science, which is therefore attributed with gratitude to God. It's another thing to know what to say of or to those suffering the same illness who receive no such rescue. On what grounds, divinely speaking, did the one receive healing and the other none whatsoever?

The intolerability of the apparent randomness with which miracles are distributed has pushed many an otherwise well-intentioned Christian into the realm of foul speculation. The healed person was a true believer, the unhealed person was not; the healed person was virtuous and possessed of great potential to serve the world, while the unhealed person was disposable and probably wicked to boot. One prayed enough and had a good prayer team behind her; the other lost confidence and got what she deserved. This one donated generously to so-and-so's ministry fundraising campaign, while that one was stingy and reaped what he sowed.

The Scriptures militate against such false inferences in both Testaments. Job's obnoxious friends are the most vivid example in the Old Testament, while Jesus' snarl of a rebuke against those who claimed to know about the souls of the victims of the Siloam tower collapse or the man born blind cut off such interpretations of disaster in the New. Positive examples of healing, for their part, often praise the faith of the patient—or even more often, the patient's intervening friends and family—but offer no corresponding commentary on theoretical neighbors who have not done the same. The Bible is no more interested in explaining randomness than demons. It is simply a hard fact of reality, even of God's own creation.

Therefore, it's safe to say that, while Western Christians do not by and large rule out the possibility of miraculous healings, we have learned to be taciturn about them and to interpret them with wary trepidation. Given the potential for corrupt and antievangelical witness, this is hardly surprising.

But here again we are challenged by Nenilava's story. You can't read it and fail to note how she calls people to repentance, casts out evil spirits, and heals illnesses—all in the same breath. We've already dealt with and dismissed the implication that affliction by evil spirits is primarily a matter of willing collaboration with them, but does Nenilava's ministry suggest that sin is at the root of all physical, emotional, and mental illness?

Careful attention to the accounts of her ministry reveals a much more nuanced picture. There is certainly no blanket equation of every single illness with a single sin as its cause. Nor is illness punishment of the sin, plain and simple. If anything, such an approach would put us squarely back in the supernature/nature paradigm, with a mechanistic correspondence between sin and illness as a causal law of "nature," which could only be interrupted by "supernature" granting forgiveness in contradiction to nature's law and justice. God's forgiveness of sins is certainly *more* than law and justice, but it is not *less* than law and justice!

Nevertheless, it's clear that when Nenilava addressed individual people, she was addressing their whole persons—and their whole persons were, of course, profoundly marked by sin. It may well be that, in a given case, illness is the outward manifestation of inward sin. Again, Westerners are more likely to invoke metaphors: "I carry stress in my lower back" or "That whole thing just made me feel sick to my stomach." Feeling the physical effects of emotional, psychological, or ethical misdeeds is no foreign experience to us. Acknowledging that does not force us to place blame for all illness solely on the guilty individual, not least of all because social and environmental sins also play a huge role in illness. Nor do we have to equate illness in every case with punishment, though in some cases we may need to acknowledge an intrinsic connection between them. (Is lung disease "punishment" for smoking, or its likely and therefore avoidable outcome?) Nenilava's approach challenges us to take up the holistic perspective and recognize healing from sin as integrated into healing from illness.

Jesus got into no small amount of trouble for making this connection—though not necessarily for the reasons that offend us nowadays. Take the healing of the paralytic in Mark 2. He was brought by concerned friends, who broke through the roof and asked for healing on the paralytic's behalf, while the paralytic himself said nothing and asked for nothing! Jesus' response to *their* faith (interestingly, not the paralytic's faith) was to say to the man: "Son, your sins are forgiven." The offended scribes took this to be blasphemous talk, but the real problem was that they took it to be *empty* talk. Jesus' subsequent healing of the paralytic's immobile legs was not only to restore the man to wholeness but also to back up the importance of the forgiveness of sins and Jesus' own authority to do so. To which the crowd responded in amazement: "We never saw anything like this before!"

The takeaway for a Western context is that we should certainly continue to guard against false inferences about a suffering person's guilt and drawing simplistic lines of connection between sin and illness. But we ought to learn from Nenilava that we may deny suffering people the chance at full restoration if we refuse altogether to speak of sin, repentance, and forgiveness in the context of healing. Addressing head-on sins committed (or experienced) may unlock vital parts of the healing process and do a world of good, even apart from any obvious sign of physical healing.

One way or another, all people are invited to repentance, in the presence of the God who forgives, before they reach the limit of all physical and mental wholeness in death. Repentance can be insisted upon at the wrong time and in the wrong way, but an authentic encounter with God will lead to repentance sooner or later. Repentance and forgiveness offer healing that persists beyond death.

Emergent Offices of Ministry

While there are clearly offices of Christian ministry named and described in the New Testament, as well as references to the laying-on of hands to confer office, there is no conclusively formulated doctrine or rite of ordination in the Bible, nor an unvarying conception of the various offices and their relationships to one another. It did not take long, of course, for the early church to begin a process of crystallizing around the assorted scriptural allusions and, in response to the very great pressures around them as well as internal challenges, to develop what would eventually become a threefold ministry of bishop/overseer, presbyter/priest/pastor, and deacon.

It was not until much, much later, when a long-established Christendom began to send missionaries to lands hitherto untouched by the gospel, that a new pressure of circumstances led to new interpretations of the same scriptural clues and apostolic mandates. In these circumstances, across countries and confessional traditions, four (at least) new offices have emerged: those of evangelist, catechist, exorcist, and Bible woman.

While the first three roles have certainly been exercised by clergy within the threefold office, the distinctive quality of these offices as they emerge in new settings is that they are directed primarily *outward*, toward the unbaptized. In theory, pastors and bishops could evangelize and catechize the masses—some certainly do, most probably do not—but their offices are not, as such, directed outward. They are inward-focused, and with good reason. Someone needs to lead the liturgy, preach, and care for the needs of the baptized; someone needs to oversee these leaders, care for them, and connect them to one another and the church farther afield. There have been many efforts to reorient the diaconate toward outward-facing service in the past century, but for most of Christian history it has functioned either as a liturgical role or as a stepping-stone toward priestly ordination. Even its reconceptualizations today tend to be oriented toward social service of one kind or another, perhaps education. Evangelism, catechization, and exorcism do not figure significantly in the present-day diaconate!

Thus, it makes good sense that distinctive outward-oriented offices of ministry should arise in settings where the basic work of evangelization has not even begun and there are significant cultural and linguistic barriers to its progress. Inevitably, foreign missionaries realize that preachers from within may be much more effective than halting and blundering outsiders. It never takes long before early converts are recruited as evangelists, to be the first contact of the gospel with locals, and catechists, who prepare converts for baptism with particular sensitivity to the obstacles and misunderstandings likely to arise and insider knowledge that no foreigner could ever hope to match.

Moreover, foreign missionaries in the past several centuries have often stumbled across places with a much livelier sense of the action of evil spirits than in their sending countries. Thus, with varying degrees of comfort, missionaries have authorized the ministry of exorcism, often undertaken by local converts, to address the needs of new or would-be believers.

The final piece of this puzzle is set in place by the Bible women, as they are almost universally known: generally unsung women who are able to access their own sex in cultures where the barrier between men and women is much higher than in missionaries' countries of origin. Bible women reach where foreign male clergy, and even foreign women, cannot. They are often among the first women of their kind to achieve literacy, but in any event they usually commit large amounts of Scripture to memory for quoting at the right time.

Readers may well be learning of these externally-oriented offices of ministry for the first time here; and it's no surprise! Lessons from the mission field are generally slow to filter back. And as long as the appearance of Christendom obtains, the need for outwardly-directed offices of ministry will not be urgently felt. But it may well be that sufficient cultural shifts have taken place in North America and Europe that the historic churches will soon be ready to recognize with greater clarity and appreciation the emergent offices of ministry in younger churches.

As for Nenilava, she seems to have embodied all four emergent offices in one person! As an evangelist, she traveled to regions where Christianity was largely unknown and called people to faith in Christ. As a catechist, she challenged indifferent church members by teaching them afresh the truths to which they had grown cold. As an exorcist, of course, she cast out the evil spirits everywhere she went. And as a Bible woman, she proclaimed and interpreted Scripture and assigned specific Bible texts to individual penitents, all according to Jesus' instruction. The only irony of the whole business is that, rather than being known primarily by any of these four offices, she has been recognized by her own church as holding of an office that is not up for grabs at all—that of prophetess!

Nenilava herself, like her three revival-founding forebears in Madagascar, necessarily stands apart somewhat from the institutional ministry of the church; her specific charism is not one to be formalized. However, as Vigen has detailed at some length, the impact of her charismatic ministry was to introduce a new form of institutional church ministry. As Vigen and I have both remarked, it is rather amazing both that she insisted on keeping her *mpiandry* attached to the formal structures of the MLC, and that the MLC in turn was willing to adopt and oversee this emergent office of ministry, especially when so many such experiments have led to new church bodies emerging altogether.

But there's no doubt that it has been a resounding success. There are thousands of *mpiandry* serving in the Ankaramalaza revival alone—a figure that does not include those in the other three revivals.[5] Each *mpiandry* undergoes rigorous training in the manner of an apprenticeship for a minimum of two years, and none ever works alone—it is always at least a pair, and more often a team, of *mpiandry* who undertake their spiritual work together. The office is consecrated by the church but not (in the technical Lutheran sense) ordained. *Mpiandry* are overseen by their local pastors, are self-funded, and by the very nature of their office enjoy a flexibility to respond to needs at hand that the inward-focused ministry simply does not.

---

5. Exact statistics are not tracked through the whole church, but the *Diary Trano* reports that in just the nine out of twenty-five synods of the MLC that actually sent in figures for the year 2020, nearly nine thousand *mpiandry* are in service! There is a total of eighty-one *toby* in operation in the Ankaramalaza revival, fifty-three of which have the right to consecrate new *mpiandry*; each of these is staffed by a number of *mpiandry* as well. Personal communication to James B. Vigen from Rakoto Endor Modeste, June 9, 2020.

It's worth mentioning that the *mpiandry*, who occupy essentially the office of exorcist though they also engage in evangelistic preaching, are not the only category of emergent office in the MLC. During my first trip to Madagascar, I asked the two hundred or so students attending the course my husband and I taught to identify for us all the offices of ministry in the MLC that were consecrated in a church rite but not ordained. They named, in addition to the *mpiandry*: evangelists, catechists, sextons (those who looked after the church property), and chaplains (for hospitals or prisons). There was some question about congregational presidents, but that category ultimately didn't seem to qualify. Between that visit and my second trip five years later, the MLC had added another category: "women theologians." A bit higher ranked than traditional Bible women, the women theologians of the MLC are permitted to wear the same clerical shirt and collar as ordained male pastors, teach, preach, exorcise, evangelize, catechize—in fact, to do pretty much everything except for the sacraments (and even baptism is allowed in a state of emergency, per ancient Christian custom).

There is no question but that the revivals of the Lutheran church in Madagascar and its consequent opening up to new and emergent offices of ministry are intimately tied both to the church's impressive growth and its remaining a part of the historic mission that founded it. In conversation with several professors of theology of the Lutheran Graduate School of Theology at Ivory, Fianarantsoa, I was surprised and impressed by the ease with which the emergent offices were integrated into their evident commitment to the Lutheran Confessions. After a long session on both the Ankaramalaza and Soatanana revivals and their resulting ministries, one of the professors patted the Book of Concord that lay near at hand and declared, "It's all in here!"

It should be stressed that, while these patterns of externally-oriented offices of ministry pop up all across the mission landscape, they are genuinely emergent. Which is to say, admiration or even envy of them doesn't suggest a quick transplant to an older Christendom setting. It may well be that new offices of externally-oriented ministry need to emerge in so-called post-Christian contexts. But they can't be forced or engineered.

Relevance for Christianity in Western Cultures

As I worked through my initial translation from the French of Tsivoery's biography, I was particularly arrested by Nenilava's account of her battle with the beast. This, too, I might have taken to be pious inflation of a heroic saint, had I not recently studied Tertullian's "The Passion of the Holy Martyrs Perpetua and Felicitas." Tertullian informs us that he is reproducing Perpetua's own handwritten account of her last days before her death in the arena. This is a vision she had while in prison:

> I gazed upon an immense assembly in astonishment. And because I knew that I was given to the wild beasts, I marveled that the wild beasts were not let loose upon me. Then there came forth against me a certain Egyptian, horrible in appearance, with his backers, to fight with me. And there came to me, as my helpers and encouragers, handsome youths; and I was stripped, and became a man. Then my helpers began to rub me with oil, as is the custom for contest; and I beheld that Egyptian on the other hand rolling in the dust. And a certain man came forth, of wondrous height, so that he even over-topped the top of the amphitheatre; and he wore a loose tunic and a purple robe between two bands over the middle of the breast; and he had on *calliculæ* of varied form, made of gold and silver; and he carried a rod, as if he were a trainer of gladiators, and a green branch upon which were apples of gold. And he called for silence, and said, "This Egyptian, if he should overcome this woman, shall kill her with the sword; and if she shall conquer him, she shall receive this branch." Then he departed. And we drew near to one another, and began to deal out blows. He sought to lay hold of my feet, while I struck at his face with my heels; and I was lifted up in the air, and began thus to thrust at him as if spurning the earth. But when I saw that there was some delay I joined my hands so as to twine my fingers with one another; and I took hold upon his head, and he fell on his face, and I trod upon his head. And the people began to shout, and my backers to exult. And I drew near to the trainer and took the branch; and he kissed me, and said to me, "Daughter, peace be with you": and I began to go gloriously to the Sanavivarian gate. Then I awoke, and perceived that I was not to fight with beasts, but against the devil. Still I knew that the victory was awaiting me.[6]

It is conceivable that Nenilava was at some point exposed to this very ancient Christian story, which dates to the beginning of the third century. Conceivable, but unlikely. And considering how late the first Christian missionaries came to Madagascar, it seems equally unlikely that the story of a remarkable woman of faith in combat with a spiritual monster circulated as a detached

---

6. Tertullian, "On the Holy Passion of the Martyrs Perpetua and Felicitas," 702.

cultural meme and reattached itself in the case of Nenilava. It seems more respectful of the evidence overall to infer that, when the gospel is first making inroads in a society that is infected with spiritual hostility to its message, it is necessary for the messengers of the gospel to undergo testing and training. That women may be called into such testing for service should not strike us as a new development but a very old tradition indeed.

Nenilava's ministry, along with the extraordinary growth it fostered in Madagascar, stands as inspiration and challenge, reassurance and warning to Christians in Western contexts.

One of the inescapable realities we face, as Vigen noted earlier in this book, is that our societies today are much less like the biblical world, or even Perpetua's, than Madagascar is. As I acknowledged above, some or many aspects of the biblical accounts may therefore strike us as absurd or strain our credulity to the breaking point; ditto the many early church stories of apostles, wonderworkers, and eccentric desert hermits. And yet—Madagascar is a place you can reach by airplane and travel about by car (admittedly, in great discomfort); and once there, you can talk to living people who knew Nenilava and saw what she did. The marvelous seems to concentrate in places where the gospel is a new arrival or where circumstances are desperate. That, too, is in keeping with gospel accounts. Nenilava's story makes the truth of these past histories at least plausible for us.

That said, we do ourselves no favors by pretending we don't live when and where we do. The Acts of the Apostles, the Pastoral Epistles, and the letters to the seven churches in Revelation, already in the first century, chart a course for a church that is figuring out how to live an apocalyptic gospel in ordinary time; how to be neither lukewarm nor hyperspiritual; how to tame, bless, and elevate such fraught matters as marriage, parenting, trade, and government in the light of Christ. If we see less of the inexplicable recoveries at the brink of death, we should not become inured to the equally great miracles of long life, health, and peace.

Therefore, Western Christians are advised not to waste time pining for a past golden era, a simpler time when people believed in God as a matter of course. Missionaries to places like Madagascar will be the first to tell you that societies like this have plenty of entrenched problems of their own, and no one need envy a place where tuberculosis and the bubonic plague are still major health threats. We are here and now, and this is God's time and place, as much as Bethlehem two thousand years ago or Ankaramalaza in the last century. We have problems unique to us; we also have countless gifts and advantages to help us tackle them. A solution from another era may spark our imagination, but it may well fail as a transplant.

Without doubt, however, just like the people in Madagascar, people in the West are afflicted by all kinds of degradation and evil; we long for healing and wholeness; we are stifled and manacled in our souls until we can confess and repent of our sins and receive forgiveness in their place. What the story of Nenilava offers us is a vivid illustration of the inbreaking of the grace of Christ against all that harms us and the new forms of Christian ministry that his grace generates to offer release from those harms—forms of ministry that are to be welcomed, disciplined, and cultivated by the church. It is Nenilava's disposition of awaiting, receiving, and extending Christ's grace that is most worthy of emulation.

Bibliography

Aano, Kjetil. "The Missions and the Fifohazana: Cultural Clashes and the Question of Power." In *The Fifohazana: Madagascar's Indigenous Christian Movement*, edited by Cynthia Holder Rich, 47–70. Amherst, NY: Cambria, 2008.

Agnes, Rasamimpianina Eveline. *Ny Tantaran'ny SALFa Sampan'Asa Loterana Momba ny Fahasalamana*. Antananarivo: TPFLM, 2019.

Allen, Philip M., and Maureen Covell, eds. *Historical Dictionary of Madagascar*. 2nd ed. Historical Dictionaries of Africa 98. Lanham: Scarecrow, 2005.

Austnaberg, Hans. *Shepherds and Demons: A Study of Excorcism as Practiced and Understood by Shepherds in the Malagasy Lutheran Church*. New York: Lang, 2008.

Bertelsen, Poul. *Design & Dignity! The Birth and Development of MSAADA Architects*. Minneapolis: Kirk, 2012.

Bleich, Erik. "Race Policy in France." https://www.brookings.edu/articles/race-policy-in-france/.

Burgess, Andrew. *Lutheran World Missions*. Minneapolis: Augsburg, 1954.

Danielson, Rajosefa. *Ny Fifohazam-pany eto Madagasikara*. Antananarivo: Volamahitsy, 1958.

Daughton, James Patrick. *An Empire Divided: Religion, Republicanism, and the Making of French Colonialism, 1880–1914*. New York: Oxford University Press, 2010.

Diary Trano Printy Fiangonana Loterana Malagasy 2020. Antananarivo: TPFLM, 2019.

Ezeanya, Stephen N. "God, Spirits and the Spirit World." In *Biblical Revelation and African Spirits*, edited by Kwesi A. Dickson and Paul Ellingworth, 30–46. Maryknoll, NY: Orbis, 1969.

Fabien, Lotera. "Malagasy Lutheran Church/Healing Ministry of Ankaramalaza." Paper given at the Lutheran Graduate School of Theology at Ivory, Fianarantsoa, 2011.

Fifohazana Miray Ao amin'ny FFPM Soatanana-Monolotrony-Ankaramalaza-Farihimena. Fitsipika Anaty. Fandaharam-pampianarana ho an ny Mpiomana ho mpiandry ["The Revival United within the FFPM. Soatanana-Manolotrony-Ankaramalaza-Farihimena. Internal Regulations. Study Guide for Those Preparing to Become Shepherds"]. 24th ed. Antananarivo: TPFLM, n.d.

Fihirana F.F.P.M. 4th ed. Antananarivo: TPFLM, 1975.

From Darkness to Light: Year Book 1938. Minneapolis: Board of Foreign Missions of the Norwegian Lutheran Church in America, 1938.

Ising, Dieter. *Johann Christoph Blumhardt, Life and Work: A New Biography*. Translated by Monty Ledford. Eugene, OR: Cascade, 2009.

Jaona, Andrianasolo, and Randriamanantena Yvonne. "The Prophet Nenilava and the Development of the Ankaramalaza Revival Movement." Translated by Mark H. Rich. In *The Fifohazana: Madagascar's Indigenous Christian Movement*, edited by Cynthia Holder Rich, 27–45. Amherst, NY: Cambria, 2008.

Jobily Faha-Dimam-polo taona ny Misiona Loterana Amerikana Fort Dauphin Madagascar, 1888–1938. Antananarivo: Friends Foreign Missionary Association, 1938.

La Liberté Religeuse à Madagascar. Paris: Maison des Missions Evangeliques, 1897.

Lisitry ny Toby miry amin'ny Fifohazana Tobilehibe Ankaramalaza. Ankaramalaza: Martsa, 2020.

Luther, Martin. *Letters of Spiritual Counsel*. Edited and translated by Theodore G. Tappert. Vancouver: Regent, 1960.

———. "Sermon on the 12th Sunday after Trinity." In *D. Martin Luthers Werke Kritische Gesamtsausgabe* 46,493,22. Weimar: Böhlau, 1967.

Mannoni, Octave. *Prospero and Caliban: The Psychology of Colonialization*. Translated by Pamela Powesland. New York: Praeger, 1964.

Melanchthon, Philip. "The Augsburg Confession." In *The Book of Concord: The Confessions of the Evangelical Lutheran Church*, edited by Robert Kolb and Timothy J. Wengert, 30–105. Minneapolis: Fortress, 2000.

Missionary Album 1926: Missionaries of the Lutheran Free Church and Views from Madagascar and China. Minneapolis: Lutheran Board of Missions, 1926.

Msaada Architects. "Lutheran Church for the Toby." https://www.msaadaarchitects.org/lutheran-church-for-the-toby.

Nielssen, Hilde, and Karina Hestad Skeie. "Christian Revivalism and Political Imagination in Madagascar." *Journal of Religion in Africa* 44.2 (2014) 189–223.

Peck, M. Scott. *People of the Lie: The Hope for Healing Human Evil*. New York: Touchstone, 1983.

Ramambason, Laurent W. *Missiology: Its Subject-Matter and Method: A Study of "Mission-Doers" in Madagascar*. New York: Lang, 1999.

"Rapports des deputes avec Ho Chi Minh: Deposition de M. Jacques Rabemananjara." In *L'insurrection malgache de 1947*, edited by Jacques Tronchon, 335–37. Fianarantsoa: Editions Ambozontany, 1982.

Rasoanahimanga, Berthe Raminosa. "Nenilava." Online Dictionary of African Christian Biography. https://dacb.org/stories/madagascar/nenilava/.

Rasolondraibe, Péri. "Healing Ministry in Madagascar." *Word & World* 9.4 (1989) 344–50.

Razato, Melchi. *Tantaran'i Nenilava sy ny Fifohazana ao Madagasikara Boky Voalohany: Soatanana, Ankaramalaza*. Self-published, CreateSpace, 2016.

Rymes, Betsy. "Names." *Journal of Linguistic Anthropology* 9.1–2 (1999) 163–66.

Shaull, Richard. Foreword to *The Pedagogy of the Oppressed*, by Paulo Freire, 9–15. New York: Seabury, 1970.

Stephenson, Rakotoarivony, et al. *Tantaran'ny Zava-Niseho Tamin'ny 02 Aogositra 1983: Fanazavan-kevitra* ["The Story of the Events of 2 August 1983: An Explanation and Clarification"]. N.p., 2004.

Taylor, John V. *The Go-Between God: The Holy Spirit and the Christian Mission*. Philadelphia: Fortress, 1972.

———. *The Primal Vision: Christian Presence amid African Religion*. London: SCM, 1963.

Tillich, Paul. *The Boundaries of Our Being: A Collection of His Sermons with His Autobiographical Sketch*. London: Collins, 1973.

Tertullian. "On the Holy Passion of the Martyrs Perpetua and Felicitas." In *Latin Christianity: Its Founder, Tertullian*, edited by Allan Menzies, 699–706. Ante-Nicene Fathers 3. Grand Rapids: Eerdmans, 1993.

Tiona sy Fihirana fanao amin'ny Fiangonana Loterana. 4th ed. Antananarivo: TPFLM, 1962.

Tobilehibe Ankaramalaza Ny Fitaran'ny Asa ["The Story of the Spiritual Work at the Ankaramalaza Toby"]. Manuscript from the Toby Ankaramalaza, 2004.

Toby Pouru Saint-Remy. "Notre Histoire." https://spflme-tobypouru.org/notre-histoire/.

Toso, Vernon. "Dear Co-Workers." *Newsletter of the American Lutheran Missionary Fellowship* (1968) 1–3.

Tronchon, Jacques, ed. *L'insurrection malgache de 1947*. Fianarantsoa: Editions Ambozontany, 1982.

Tronchon, Jacques, and James B. Vigen. "Dynamisme ecclesial et affrontements (1896–1913)." In *Madagascar et le Christianisme*, edited by Bruno Hübsch, 325–48. Paris: Editions Karthala, 1993.

Tsivoery, Zakaria. "L'Histoire du Réveil d'Ankaramalaza (1941–1970)." In *Ankaramalaza. Germaine Volahavana Nenilava. Histoire et Temoignages*, 9–70. Antananarivo: TPFLM, 2006.

———. "Ny Tantaran' Ankaramalaza." In *Ny Tantaran'y Fifohazana eto Madagasikara: Soatanana, Farihimena, Ankaramalaza*, 172–265. Antananarivo: TPFLM, 1972.

Ulrich, Carl L. "An Examination of Possible Animistic Practices in the Revival Movement." MTh thesis, Luther Seminary, 1972–73.

Vigen, James B. *Diakonia: A Short History of Manambaro Lutheran Hospital*. Antananarivo: TPFLM, 1979.

———. "A Historical and Missiological Account of the Pioneer Missionaries in the Establishment of the American Lutheran Mission in Southeast Madagascar." PhD diss., Lutheran School of Theology at Chicago, 1991.

Wengert, Timothy J., and Philip D. W. Krey. "A June 1546 Exorcism in Wittenberg as a Pastoral Act." *Archive for Reformation History* 98 (2007) 71–83.

Zahl, Simeon. *Pneumatology and Theology of the Cross in the Preaching of Christoph Friedrich Blumhardt*. Edinburgh: T&T Clark, 2012.

www.ingramcontent.com/pod-product-compliance
Lightning Source LLC
Chambersburg PA
CBHW070918160426

43193CB00011B/1508